The Jerusalem Community
Rule of Life

The Jerusalem Community
Rule of Life

FOREWORD BY CARLO CARRETTO

Paulist Press

Published in the USA in 1985 by Paulist Press,
997 Macarthur Boulevard, Mawah,
N. J. 07430

Published in Great Britain by
Darton, Longman and Todd, London as
A City Not Forsaken

Translation © 1985 Darton, Longman and Todd Ltd

The English translation was made by Sister Kathleen England
from the French *Jerusalem: Livre de Vie* by Pierre-Marie
Delfieux published and © by Les Editions du Cerf 1981

ISBN 0–8091–2712–1

Phototypeset by Input Typesetting Ltd, London SW19 8DR
Printed and bound in Great Britain by
Anchor Brendon Ltd, Tiptree, Essex

Contents

Foreword

It is no hardship for me to introduce this book by
Pierre-Marie Delfieux. If you live a long time together
in the desert, it doesn't take much to find yourselves
sharing your thoughts, feelings and ideals.

I met Pierre-Marie at Beni Abbes and was carried
away by his youth and the warmth of his love for God.
I couldn't have imagined a truer or more valuable
companion.

With him, I travelled the trails, saw him building
the stone hermitages of Baba-aïda. With him, I prayed
in desert chapels and, with him, was uplifted in the
liturgy when we met on feast-days to celebrate the
Eucharist.

We were both in love with God and the empty
places, and our dreams coincided to the very depths
of our being.

Our paths continually intersected in common
ideals, to the point where I would willingly have lived
Pierre-Marie's life, and he mine.

In the desert we had discovered the Divine Absolute, and problems were no more, including that of
bridging the gap between city and desert.

For there was no gap: the desert was no longer
absence of men, but presence of God.

And this presence may be felt as well out there in
the sands as in the modern city.

Delfieux chose the city and went to Paris, where he
pitched his tent. But his heart was in the desert.

I chose the desert sands, but my heart was in the
city.

With Pierre-Marie's project in mind, I wrote the
book *The Desert in the City*[1], explaining what a fine

[1] Published by Collins, 1979.

thing founding the monastic Fraternities of Jerusalem would be.

The root was the same, and we were consciously united in the same cause.

Every evening at the hour of incense, I found myself, in spirit, saying Vespers with him in Paris, while he, in spirit, joined me 'in silent prayer and adoration' at Our Lady of the Dunes in Beni Abbes.

I believe the Family of Jerusalem has a great future in fulfilling the dream that has always been mine, of quickening the modern city with the freshness of prayer.

Grandiose, the design; fiery, its moving spirit.

Enough of this . . .

The desert trail leads through the city now, summoning man to contemplate the mystery of the Absolute God.

BROTHER CARLO CARRETTO

Introduction

Writing as an Anglican monk, endeavouring to live by the Spirit of the Rule of St Benedict in semi-rural England, I may seem to be distanced in many ways from Father Pierre-Marie Delfieux and the Fraternities of Jerusalem in the heart of Paris.

Yet there is only one Spirit of Life and Unity, and only one Faith, one Lord, one Baptism. Wherever we are, Christian monks are engaged in the same search for God, for Christ. Today particularly we are all searching and working for a full communion with our Christian brothers and sisters 'that the world may believe'. We search also for a full communion with God our Father and for the coming of his Kingdom among the poor and the dispossessed of our day.

The English translation of the Rule of Life written by Father Pierre-Marie for the Jerusalem Community, offers to each one of us a practical hand-book for this shared search, both for a lived, full communion among Christians, and for God where he is least expected: in the noise, tumult and anonymity of the modern city and in those who are increasingly becoming the casualties of our society. If the insights and teaching found in this Rule were applied and lived in new communities throughout the English-speaking world, the work of Christian unity and witness would be advanced.

The Monastic Fraternities of Jerusalem are two closely associated communities in Paris, one for monks and one for nuns, founded respectively in 1975 and 1976, and new communities are in preparation. The original communities have the use of the Church of St Gervais in the centre of the city of Paris. Their life is adapted to the needs of the city today, and the Church authorities have commissioned them to be a 'space of silence', an oasis amid the city bustle. Their vocation is not pastoral but monastic, and their life is composed of the various requirements of fraternal life; common and private prayer, part-time work, silence and openness, under a promise of poverty, chastity and obedience. They are in the city 'in search for God alone', but living in true solidarity with men. If Paris is Babel, it is also the Holy City, for God lives in it and we want to contemplate him there. Jerusalem is the city where Jesus lived, prayed, gave witness and died before he rose again.

Thus, although the roots of the Jerusalem Community are in the desert tradition and the desert experience of the founder, the life is lived in the city and for the city. The communities worship together three times a day, at 7.30 a.m., 12.30 p.m. and 5.30 p.m., and the two periods of corporate prayer in the morning and evening are arranged for the needs of the city-people as much as for the convenience of the Fraternities. One day a week the monks and nuns retreat to the 'desert' outside Paris for a day of prayer and refreshment in the spirit of solitude.

These new Fraternities have several characteristics which together mark them out as a new departure. In addition to living in the city, the monks and nuns are wage-earners five mornings a week, both in order to earn money on which to live and to be in solidarity with other workers in the city. They are tenant-occupiers, and with this poor, mobile and adaptable. Not strictly enclosed, they have a greater contact with the people of the city; and living directly under the jurisdiction of the local bishop they are more firmly rooted in the life and witness of the local church.

The Fraternities have several forms of membership. There are brothers in community, sisters in community, solitaries, family group members and lay Fraternities. Many and varied as they are, they bear the same name and live in a common spirit of the Rule of Life. 'In the heart of the city' they live 'in the heart of God'.

Rooted in the reality of the city today, and yet springing from the tradition of the desert, the Prior, Father Pierre-Marie Delfieux, has been inspired to write this adventurous new Rule for the community he has nurtured into existence. This English translation will enable many more to pray and reflect upon the possibilities for our own countries, whether to stimulate new action and thought in existing communities or to encourage the emergence of fresh Jerusalem Fraternities in our cities.

The Rule itself sets the Jerusalem Fraternities in the evolving tradition of French monasticism. The Fraternities have much in common with the inspiring but severe life at the Benedictine monasteries of Fleury and La Pierre qui Vire, with the new urban communities of St Jean founded by Father Marie-Dominique Philippe O.P., with the Little Brothers and Sisters of Charles de Foucauld, with the Benedictine Community of St Benoît de Banlieue, and with the teaching of the Carmelite Sister Elizabeth of the Trinity. This variety of inspiration is reflected in the references and sources of the Rule and gives it an altogether new character. However, as well as drawing upon current French Roman Catholic thought, the Rule also has a strong Orthodox character. There are more references of St Basil than to St Benedict, and many to the Desert Fathers. The liturgy has a strong Orthodox influence both in ceremonial and music, as well as the church furnishing, making it an easy and joyful experience in which to participate. The Fraternities have also been influenced by the openness and spontaneity of the charismatic renewal.

Perhaps the beginnings of a monastic renewal are already visible in the English-speaking world. It is hoped that the renewal to come will incorporate much of what is now to be seen in the Jerusalem Fraternities. It may even be possible to pioneer an ecumenical community along similar lines. There have already been practical experiments in living in this new way in the city. Within the Anglican Diocese of Southwark in South London a series of community weeks were held from 1980–2 at St Peter's, Vauxhall. Also in London, the Benedictine Monastery of St Peter in East Dulwich, opened in 1984, is a more permanent expression of a similar ideal. The many Taizé-style groups and basic communities meeting for common worship and witness all over the world, the several lay Fraternities of Jerusalem in Europe, America and Australia, and the joint Anglican-Roman Catholic Monastery of the Incarnation in Berkeley, California, all bear witness to the same movement in the Church, as does the Columbanus Community in Belfast. I hope that the publishing of this Rule of Life will encourage those involved in Christian community living to explore such new patterns of monastic living for Christian unity and witness in the city.

The Rule of Life is aimed at all Christians. It is clearly divided into three sections; on Fraternity, for all those who are seeking; on Monasticism, for those who seek a closer commitment; and on Jerusalem, which points to the contemplation of God in the city and its fulfilment in Christ. So the Rule is applicable to family groups and lay communities as well as to the Monastic Fraternities since it meets many of the needs of any Christian who lives in a city. A new orientation to the world is given in corporate worship, a shared life of the local community, and an emphasis on the personal relationship of the believer with his Saviour and his neighbour. In this way the Rule of Life has a universal application as well as a relevance and immediacy to those drawn to community living. And, for Christians committed to working and praying for unity, the Rule has real potential as a force for ecumenism.

The Rule of Life is, I believe, a resource providing for Christians a way into the Christian life of the future through the religious and social turmoil of the present. It will help to carry into a new age the treasures and insights of the past, as did the Rule of St Benedict nearly fifteen hundred years ago.

DOM JAMES LEACHMAN O.S.B.
Monk of Nashdom Abbey

Preface

In the name of the Father and of the Son and of the Holy Spirit, Amen!

To you, brothers and sisters, grace and peace from our Father and the Lord Jesus Christ!

Eph. 1:2

Who am I, sinful and mortal man that I am, to offer you a Book of Life whose sole aim is to lead us all together to sanctity?

But since God wants it this way, I cannot well refuse to serve as the useless tool he always prefers, and try to put our Rule of Life into adequate words, since all of us have agreed this to be both a necessary and good thing, as we learn from the example of the saints and our own reason, in the Lord Jesus Christ.[1]

Acts 9:15
Luke 17:10

With some trepidation then, listening to the Holy Spirit, I have set to work, convinced I had nothing of myself to give but everything to receive from God; simply to try and set down clearly, what our way of life and actual situation is, upheld by your trust and prayer. And throughout all these days I have felt this strength distinctly and deeply. Days of solitary prayer and silence during which I have tried to receive on my knees, from Scripture and Tradition, what God himself has already put into our hearts and our lives.

Deut. 30:14

All along I have tried as far as possible to say nothing but what the Lord has already shown and commanded us, basing myself on Holy Scripture and the living remembrance of Christ, with the inner voice of the Spirit leading and illuminating everything; and on the Church's perennial practice and teaching, as well as on what we have already experienced and verified together.

---

[1] cf. Ignatius Loyola, *Constitutions of the Society of Jesus*, prologue.

So, it seemed good to remind ourselves of the essential why and wherefore on which our daily life depends; stressing our great Trinitarian Exemplar and the Face of Christ, perfect pattern of any life of charity, prayer, work, silence and hospitality, and unique model of poverty, chastity, obedience, humility and joy.

It seemed equally necessary and good, too, to look for support in this vocation by remembering what so many holy monks and nuns and our Fathers in the Faith have already written, or lived, along the same lines and for the same end; and, as far as possible, keeping in mind the Blessed Virgin Mary to whom our Fraternities are consecrated.

Practically speaking, I thought I should best express a direct, simple and personal dialogue by writing in the second person; not between myself and each of you, but between the Lord speaking immediately, simply and personally to each one of us, a style used by the greater number of monastic rules and in biblical and liturgical dialogue. I have deliberately avoided using inverted commas and have placed references in the margin[2] or footnotes so as the better to express what comes from the Lord, enabling you to refer to it as you like.

So now let us welcome this Book of Life together. More than a Rule properly speaking, it is a *spiritual outline* containing the main orientations of our way of life; sufficiently precise to guide our footsteps and to make of our lives one harmonious whole. Pray over it, accept and practise it, in humility and truth with fervour and obedience.

The worth of a Rule lies not so much in what it says in words as in the life lived by it. Not lived, a beautiful Rule is merely a dead letter. Well lived, an imperfect Rule becomes spirit and life. It is not those who listen to the law who are righteous in God's sight but those who put it into practice.

Rom. 2:13
Luke 11:28

May God pardon the imperfections of word or

---

[2] The *biblical* references to the ideas expressed in each paragraph are set in the margin and grouped at the end of the relevant paragraph is sequential order.

thought in this Book of Life, and may he give us the grace to take it really and totally to heart, to supply by the perfection of our lives what is lacking in the perfection of expression.

No longer serving in the old way of a written code but in newness of the Spirit.   Rom. 7:6

The grace of the Lord Jesus be with you.

My love to you all in Christ Jesus.   1 Cor. 16:23–4

FATHER PIERRE-MARIE DELFIEUX

13 rue des Barres   *Prior of Jerusalem*
75004 Paris   *Paris, 29 June 1978*

FRATERNITIES

1   Love

1   Love.

Open your whole being to the love of God with which God first loved you. Anchor yourself forever in this certitude, the only one that gives meaning, strength and joy to your life: his love for you will never go away nor his covenant of peace with you ever be overthrown. God's gifts and his calls are irrevocable. He has engraved your name on the palms of his hands.

1 John 4:19
Isa. 54:10
Rom. 11:29
Isa. 49:16

Let your soul be filled day and night with this loving presence of the Lord, and you will live. Strong in the joy of this divinity within you and the power of his love, you will never falter.

Ps. 119:55,77
Isa. 26:9

By faithfully treasuring all these things in your heart like Mary, you will gradually be invaded, built up and unified by God. Always to be open to his love is the first duty of your consecration.

2   With the strength of this grace, *return the love of your whole heart, and soul, all your strength and spirit to the Lord* who created you in his image and likeness. In a word, love him with your whole self and your entire life. Your monastic vocation consists in the totality of this undivided love.

Gen. 1:27
Luke 10:27

Knowing he has loved you by giving you his whole life, your only return can be to give him yours. So great was his love that he gave you his only Son, and you have chosen to make a free gift of the only life you have. Your entire self-offering to Love for love will spur you on to accept the loss of all things to gain Christ. And then you will learn that everything is

John 3:16

Phil. 3:8
1 Cor. 3:23 nothing and nothing everything.[1] For if everything is yours, you are Christ's and Christ is God's.

You will indeed be a monk or nun, if your gaze is fixed on God alone, on God alone your desire and concentration. And wanting to serve God alone, at peace with him, you will be a source of peace to others.[2]

3 If your whole life is a free, joyous *welcoming* of his love and a laborious, patient *seeking* of his face, alone with the One, you will be able to stand before him like a true son, and in your heart the Spirit of
Gal. 4:6 his only Son will cry out: Abba! Father!

Since you have acknowledged God, or rather, he has acknowledged you, if you love him, keep his Word; and the Father will love you, and God-One-
Gal. 4:9
John 14:23 in-Three will come into you and make you his dwelling-place.

Then you will be able to say, you no longer live but God lives in you, and you will be the living tent of
Gal. 2:20
1 Cor. 3:17 his presence. Truly consecrated. For that temple is sacred, and you are that temple.

Everything you will have to do in the monastic life is designed to lead you precisely to that point. God is a devouring fire wanting to consume you utterly in his love. May the words the Lord is saying to you
Heb. 12:29
Deut. 6:6
Luke 10:28 today remain deep in your heart. Do this and you will live.

4 Love your brothers and sisters.

Tread the way of love like Christ. How can you
Eph. 5:2
1 John 4:20 profess to love God whom you do not see, if you do not love the brother or sister just beside you?

Since charity is the fullness of the law, the demands of fraternal love sum up your whole monastic life, just as they do the law and the prophets. Question yourself at every moment about your love, for by love you will
Rom 13:10 be judged.[3]

[1] St Theresa of Avila.
[2] St Theodore the Studite.
[3] St John of the Cross.

4

Since in heaven we shall do nothing but love, eternally and totally; and the monk tries to *anticipate* the kingdom;

1 John 4:16

Since God is love as Jesus made plain, and the monk wants to *imitate* Christ;

Rom. 5:8
John 15:12–13

Since the first commandment is to love and the monk *obeys* God by doing his will and nothing else;

Mark 12:29

Love untiringly, undividedly, without a murmur. May the Lord cause you to grow and abound in love towards all men.

1 Thess. 3:12

> Here, once and for all, you have been given this short precept;
> Love and do what you will.
> If you keep silence, let it be for love.
> If you speak, let it be for love.
> If you correct a brother, correct for love.
> If you pardon, pardon for love.
> Cherish the root of love in the depth of your heart.
> From this root nothing but good can come.[4]

5   Accept the fact, however, that you tend naturally to what is less good. Gaze lucidly into the depths of your egocentric, egoistic, jealous, aggressive, insinuating self, and see the devil there criticizing your brothers, seeking at all times someone to devour, sowing bad seed under cover of darkness.

Rev. 12:10
1 Pet. 5:8
Matt. 13:25

To be open to love, you have continually to turn away from self-love. Without this preliminary stance of humility and conversion you will never learn *to* love.

The more you learn *to love yourself* the better you will learn to love your brothers.

Lev. 19:18

If you are unified you will be unifying; pacified you will pacify. Love yourself humbly and boldly and from there set out to love your neighbour as yourself. This is the second essential for loving your fellowman.

Love yourself to the point of self-forgetfulness.

There is receiving love, sharing love, giving love

---

[4] St Augustine, *Commentary on 1 John 7:8.*

and self-giving love. And finally, the love of self-immolation. Monk and nun, God expects even that. If one day you can say that all your self-seeking has come to an end, you will live the happiest of lives possible,[5] and through you God's love will shine. This is the third essential for loving your fellow-man.

6 Every day ask God to pour love for your brothers into your heart and to put love for you into theirs. God can deny nothing to a community that prays this way, because it is his will that we love one another as he has loved us.

John 15:12–17

Where there is no love, put love and you will harvest love.[6] Susceptibility is charity's worst enemy, humility its best ally. You should be intelligent and holy enough to be the first to give way in a quarrel; and never let squabbles over trifles harm your deep union with your brothers. You may be in the right, but your duty is not to let the sun go down on your anger. Resolve each day anew to pray for your brothers. Pray that you may love, and love while you pray, and the grace of his love will find a way in.

Eph. 4:26
1 Thess.
3:12–13

Look on the call to brotherly love as the entry into an immense mystery, since it is your gateway into God himself. Where love is, there is God. You, with your brethren, give God a body, express his presence and signify his action. Let your whole community become in this way a theophany of his love.

1 John 4:16

7 To express this love in authentic action, you must live *sharing*. Share your time, table, roof, salaries, and belongings. Possess nothing so that one day you may, like Christ, be enriched by all you have given away. Likewise, you should be able to say to each community member: all that is mine is yours.

1 John 3:18
2 Cor. 8:9
Luke 15:31

Your journey to Christ is not a solitary, but a communal, project. It is a shared commitment that

5 St Teresa of Lisieux.
6 St John of the Cross.

6

implies listening and encouraging each other, brotherly conversion, bound up in the same gift.

Bear one another's burdens and you will fulfill the law of Christ. In all humility, gentleness and patience, bear with one another in charity.

Gal. 6:2
Eph. 4:2

You enter the Fraternity to share everything: from the slightest detail to the most basic commitment, and in so doing you and your brethren build up the living body of the only Son. So that all of us united with Christ form one body, serving as limbs and organs to one another. If that is your aim and you live it, the joy of sharing will blot out the memory of the sacrifices.

Rom. 12:5
John 16:21–3

8   With your brothers and sisters and all the variety of their gifts of grace, strive to build up *unity* in *diversity*. But never forget that the climb to unity is harder going than the slide into diversity. If your unity is strong you will be inventive and creative in diversity.

Rom. 12:6
1 Cor. 12
Eph. 4:3–13

For fear unity should turn into a shapeless amalgam or a mechanical conformity, or diversity become self-centred individualism or eccentric fantasy, beg God-One-in-Three to reveal to you the secret of his unity in plurality.

John 17:21

Let the unity of your Fraternity manifest your shared love.

Let the mature personality of each of your brothers demonstrate his freedom. Whether you pray, study or work, be glad someone else is working, studying and praying for you.[7] All these gifts are the work of one and the same Spirit, distributing them separately to each individual at will.

1 Cor. 12:11

9   To be able to love, be *open*.

Let yourself be known and try to get to know others. Of necessity, knowledge leads to love. By being open of heart, of action and thought, you will the better learn how to fit in with your brothers and overcome the devil's wiles; do not let Satan take you

---

[7] Pseudo-Macarius, *The Cenobitical Life*, 3rd homily.

2 Cor. 2:11
John 3:21

in. Be aware of his plans. The man who acts in the truth comes to the light.

Be humble enough to let yourself be seen for what you really are, and understanding enough to see without judging. This twofold effort will show you

Gal. 6:1–10
Ps. 133:1

what a good and happy thing it is for brothers to live together.

Forever banish backbiting, murmuring and jealousy from your lips and heart. Flee petty argument between brothers. Nothing is more divisive than endless discussions about everything and anything. Know how to put an end to this. Refuse to listen to gossip about this or that brother. Be a leaven of unity . . .[8] The man who slanders his neighbour in secret I shall silence . . . No place in my house for the man

Ps. 101:5–7

who practises deceit.

Never say or listen to anything about an absent brother that you have not already said or are prepared to say to his face.

And pray that monastic fraternity as a whole may be sincere in the presence of the Word as a source of

Phil. 2:15

light and a living icon of the Trinity.

10

Col. 3:13
Eph. 4:27–32
Luke 6:36
Matt. 6:12
Luke 17:3

Never tire of *forgiving*, and so give the devil no hold. Be merciful and compassionate, spontaneously and wholeheartedly. The Lord forgives you all day long; in the silence of your heart, then, do the same, untiringly and sincerely.

Matt. 18:35

Should you have some special cause for complaint against anyone, go at once and make friends again in mutual forgiveness. If that does not work, tell the prior, who will consider with you what is to be done to reconcile you and this brother; should that still not be enough, then call a few of the brothers; after that put the matter before the community; let all then put their trust in the mercy of God and the judgement of

Col. 3:15

the Holy Spirit.

If anyone is unwilling to love and forgive sincerely, then he should neither enter nor remain in the

Matt. 18:15.18

monastic life.

[8] *Rule of Taizé.*

8

With complete freedom, as your conscience bids, receive the grace of sacramental penance from your confessor in agreement with your prior. Without a spiritual father it is difficult to advance along the way of perfection.

Once a week, in the presence of God, live the grace of *mutual forgiveness*, according to the word of the apostle who urges us to confess our sins to one another. This communal absolution strengthens the bonds of that Fraternity, enabling each brother to grow in light and truth.

Jas. 5:16

Whenever you are asked, be willing to share brotherly exhortation with your brothers; it will be a call to conversion and a source of strength to you.

11 It is not enough to say you are everyone's brother; you should be his *friend* too. Make a friend of each brother without insisting that he be yours as well. This is what Christ meant when he called us to be friends instead of servants. Authentic friendship expands, liberates, dynamizes and matures. But a friendship that is too human or exclusive is stunting, divisive and in the end becomes a burden. A kind of friendship you should cultivate is the first and you should be fiercely on your guard against the second.

John 15:15
Luke 12:4
Ecclus.
6:14–17

Above all live AS ONE BODY. It is the vital source of our living, chosen in Christ before the creation of the world; and it is the goal of the call that has gathered us into one body. At the heart of this broken world, may unity of charisms build us up into a holy temple, and diversity of members mould us into a single cohesive body. Then with your brothers at the heart of the city, you will be clothed in charity which is perfection, the sign of brotherly communion and, hence, pure splendour of God. Such is the glory he has granted you to share with him.

Eph. 1:4
Col. 3:15
Eph. 4:16
John 17:22

May this be the sign by which the world we live in—although we no longer belong to it—may recognize us as his disciples: the love we have for one another.

John 13:55

9

2 Prayer

12

Luke 11:1
Pray.

As Jesus did, do you also pray.

His whole life was turned towards the Father in unceasing offering, listening, inner melodies of adoration, love, thanksgiving and perpetual intercession for men. Prayer so unified him and united him to God that he could say he was in the Father and the Father in him. In this sense, he is the perfect monk and, John 14:10–11 hence, for you the unique model.

Outwardly, he chose special places and times to intensify and manifest his prayer: in the temple, on the mountain, in the wilderness, away from the crowd, or simply some odd spot during the day or along the road. By day and by night, alone or with his disciples, he was always praying.[1]

Through this unceasing love-relationship and these special times and places, his filial love grew greater John 12:45–6; 14:9 and the light of his holiness shone forth. Seeing him, people could see the Father.

Do, brother or sister, son or daughter of the same Father, if you want to know how, why or where to pray, fix your eyes on Jesus and do as he did, because Luke 11:1 only he can teach you how to pray.

When he called you to the monastic life, he invited you to dedicate yourself completely to this essential task for which you have consented to leave all. When you became a monk you chose to make your whole life a prayer and prayer your life. The whole aim of

---

[1] Biblical references for this paragraph in sequence: Luke 2:41; Matt. 21:12; John 2:14; Matt. 5:1; Luke 6:12; 9:28; Mark 3:13; 1:45; Luke 5:16; Matt. 14:13; Luke 11:1; 6:12; Matt. 26:36; Luke 9:18; 3:21.

a monk and the perfection of his heart consist in uninterrupted steadfastness in prayer.[2]

Mark 10:28

13 The *Holy Spirit* is the master of your prayer vocation. Even if you can do nothing more than ask to pray as you ought, the Spirit himself will come to the help of your weakness, intercede for you and teach you the right way to pray.

Rom. 8:26

Believe that the love of God has been poured into your heart by the Holy Spirit who has been given to you and that, consequently, you are no longer slave but son and heir in God's name to all the promises of divine glory. So when you pray, pray in the Holy Spirit. And never stifle his inspiration. The Father cannot refuse to give him to you if only you ask.

Rom. 5:5
Jude 20
1 Thess. 5:19
Luke 11:13

It is in prayer that you meet God, speak and listen to him and receive and respond to his love.

Prayer brings you self-knowledge and maturity; it lights up your path and strengthens your heart.

Prayer enables you to understand and relate more easily to others, to help them wholeheartedly and reach your highest point of usefulness in this world.

For the sake of God, the world and yourself, keep watch and pray without ceasing. Nothing is more marvellous for a man than to give himself up to contemplation.

Luke 21:36

14 By choosing to pray *at the heart of the city*, you mean to show that your life is centred in God. Urban monasticism is not there for solidarity, apostolate or even witness. Your priority is to contemplate God freely and incessantly in the most beautiful of all his images. That is, more than in solitude, on the mountains, or in the wilderness or the temple, you gaze on him in the city of men, being faces of the face of God and mirrors of the icon of Christ. Monk and nun of Jerusalem, you are at the heart of the city of God.

Gen. 1:27
Ezek. 48:35
Isa. 60:14

But your choice led you to unification rather than separation of prayer and life. To bring your prayer

[2] John Cassian, *Conferences* IX:2.

right into the city and to receive the city into your prayer. To live the link between action and contemplation, work and contemplation, the street and contemplation. As Jesus and Mary and the apostles and so many monks have done before you. Their example should be your hope and support.

15 Prayer is *difficult*: that you know. It is the very spot where your free giving takes place; the abode of the invisible, often of the unfelt, the incomprehensible, the ineffable, the unexpected. For you too, it will be hard to love a God whose face you have never seen.[3] And your prayer will be a fight to the last gasp.[4] In this sense, God has armed your hands for combat and shielded your head for the day of battle. Fight the good fight of faith, then, conquer eternal life to Ps. 140:8 which you are called and to gain which you have made 1 Tim. 6:12 your splendid profession of monastic faith.

Do not place your happiness in what you can hear or feel of God in prayer but rather in what you can neither feel nor understand. . . God is always hidden and difficult to find. Go on serving him in this way, as though he were concealed in a secret place, even when you think you have found him, felt him or heard him. The less you understand the closer you get to him.[5] Prayer will show you that God is forever the Wholly Other, and you will always fall short.

Prayer will teach you, too, that he is nearer to you than you are to yourself.[6] After passing the fiery crucible and stepping through the narrow doorway 1 Cor. 3:15 Matt. 7:14; 6:21 of your heart that contains him whom the whole uni- Ecclus. 7:5 verse cannot hold.

In prayer, then, you will find *peace, light and joy*. There will be the source of your love and the strength of your life. To enlighten your mind, pray. To discern your path, pray. To unify your being, pray. That light may fall on your face and rejoice your heart, pray. To

[3] St Teresa of Avila.
[4] Abba Agathon.
[5] St John of the Cross.
[6] St Augustine.

12

be incorporated into Christ, pray: you no longer live but Christ lives in you. Gradually you will be enlightened, cleansed, purified, matured and joyfully quickened. And so, deified. Filled with your fullness you will be able to enter God's total plenitude. Nothing is left but to contemplate his glory.

2 Cor. 3:18
Gal. 2:20
Eph. 3:19
John 17:24

16   Along this road with its struggles and its glory, you will come to learn all the secrets of prayer.

Pray like a poor man. You are fragile, wayward, distracted, radically incapable of reaching God and receiving him. You are a sinner faced with the Thrice Holy God. Accept your poverty, knowing that Jesus blessed the prayer of the humble tax-collector. The prayer of the poor man rises to the ears of God.

Luke 18:14
Ecclus. 21:5

Pray like a child. Beloved, even now you are God's children. Only if you become a little child can you enter his kingdom. Heaven will be yours only if you believe with all a child's faith. Let the song of little children rise to your lips. Child of God, led by God's Spirit, yours will be a share in the holy liberty of the children of God.

1 John 3:2
Matt. 18:3
Mark 10:14
Ps. 8:3
Rom. 8:14,21

Pray in the name of Jesus. Be sons in the Son, and the Father will be unable to refuse you anything. Perhaps you have never yet asked in his name? Ask and you will receive and your joy will be full. All you ask in his name, Jesus will do and the Father will grant it. The all-powerfulness of the Trinity dwells in the man who believes, and still more in the man who loves, and for him everything is possible. So if you love and believe, your prayer in the name of Jesus will make you capable of anything whatever.

John 16:27,24;
14:13; 15:16
Mark 9:23
John 14:23

17   *Pray in the Holy Spirit.* Now that you have the Spirit of God living in you and you have received the spirit of adopted sons by which you cry: Abba, Father, let him come to you in the depths of your weakness to intercede for you himself with inexpressible groans. By prayer, become docile to the revealer of all truth, who will overwhelm you with his fruitfulness. Since

Rom. 8:9.15

13

John 16:13
Gal. 5:22–5

the Spirit is your life, may the Spirit praying in you spur you to action.

Pray trustfully. You do not realize the power your prayer exerts over God's heart. The fervent prayer of a good man is very strong. Christ has said so over and over again: All you ask when you pray, believe you have received it already and it will be given to you.

Jas. 5:16
Mark 11:24

Pray steadfastly. Joyfully hopeful, constant under trial, be assiduous in prayer. If you are vigilant in thanksgiving, your steadfastness, however importunate it becomes, will be heard. Because of your insistence God will arise and give you all you need.

Rom. 12:12
Col. 4:2
Luke 18:1–8;
11:8

18   *Pray bravely.* There will be plenty of hurdles. From the devil first, who prowls round like a roaring lion, looking for someone to devour; and then those endless outside interferences and your own innate laziness. Recall the prophet's promise: Courage, children. Pray to God and he will snatch you from the violence of your enemies. Your effort will be followed by peace.

1 Pet. 5:8
Baruch 4:21–7

Prayer should be more intense at *turning points in your life*, when you have to take decisions, face difficulties and temptations or deal with misunderstandings; it was what Jesus did. Be on the alert and pray at all times for strength to pass safely through imminent troubles so as to stand upright in the presence of the Son of Man.

Luke 21–36

Pray temperately and simply. Prayer is a heart-to-heart talk between yourself and God and needs no brilliant ideas, no flood of words. Gradually you should come to pure and simple listening to the One who has the words of eternal life.

John 6:68

Pray in secret. All that counts in you is the fact of God's presence nurtured by your personal and solitary prayer. When you pray, go into your cell, close the door, and pray to your Father who is there in secret, and your Father who sees in secret will be near you.

Matt. 6:6

Pray with your brothers. Be convinced that where two or three are gathered in his name, Jesus is in their midst and the spirit is specially close to shared prayer

Matt. 18:19

14

The Father greatly loves to grant the common prayer of the brothers assembled round his only Son!

Acts 2:1–4
John 15:7–16

19 In short, strive to *pray continually and tirelessly*. Set the Lord always before your eyes, as the psalmist did; and like the wise man ever pondering the commandments of the Lord, be joyful and pray without ceasing, thankful always; which is God's will for you in Christ Jesus.

Luke 18:1
Ps. 16:8
Ecclus. 6:37
1 Thess.
5:16–18

Venerate and honour him whom you believe to be the Word and, through him, the Father. Such is your duty. Not at certain special times as others do but continually, all your life long and in every way . . . Prayer is an intimate exchange with God and God is always listening to this inward voice . . . Indeed, the truly spiritual man prays all his life long, since to pray, for him, is to strive after union with God, and he casts aside all useless burdens, since he has already reached the state in which he has to some degree received that perfection which consists in acting through love. His whole life is one long sacred liturgy. . .[7]

When all your love, all your desire, all your efforts, all your search, all your thought, all you live for and speak of and all you breathe is God alone, when the unity of the Father with the Son and the Son with the Father has passed into your soul and heart,[8] then you will experience the unutterable joy of continuous prayer and your life will be life indeed!

20 Pray with your brothers *in the morning*, before you go to work and with those setting out to work; repeating to yourself: I rise before the dawn and I cry: Lord, I hope in your word!

Ps. 119:147

Pray *at midday* while you are at work, with those at work, at the sixth hour when Jesus offered his life for you and for the salvation of the world.

Matt. 27:45

Pray *in the evening*, with those coming back from

[7] Clement of Alexandria, *Stromateis*, VII:7.
[8] John Cassian, op. cit. X:6, 7.

15

work, as night draws on, at the beginning of the vigils,
and turn everything into thanksgiving—Eucharist.

Lam. 2:19

This should be your liturgy, bringing you and your
brothers into your church, before God, three times a
day. Daniel had windows made in his roof chamber
looking towards Jerusalem, and there he knelt down
three times a day and offered prayer and praises to
his God as his custom had always been.

Dan. 6:10

21   Every week, on Thursdays, remember Geth-
semane, where there was no one to pray for an hour
with Jesus, and *pray in the night* in the midst of the
joys and miseries of the city, where God has placed
you like a watchman watching for the dawn. Beg
forgiveness for your own sins and thank God for his
marvels; rise in the middle of the night to thank him
for his just judgements. The Church has called us to
be the watchmen to alert the people, and to be awake
on the city ramparts. You too, get up in the night at
the beginning of the vigils to pour out your heart like
water before the Lord your God.

Mark 14:37
Isa. 21:11
Ps. 130:6;
119:62
Isa. 62:6
1 Thess. 5:5–6
Lam. 2:19

Every afternoon, meditate on the Scriptures, and
let the Spirit himself shape in you a disciple's spirit
in spiritual reading and open your heart wide to the
joy of his divine presence as Christ promised: if
anyone loves me, we will come to him and make our
abode in him. Your cell will turn into an oratory,
where you will find the secret of your happiness:
blessed is the man who delights in the law of the Lord
and murmurs his law by day and by night.

John 14:23
Ps. 119:97

22   Prayer will then turn you into a *man of the liturgy*.
It is an urban monk's calling. With the psalmist you
will thank God in the great assembly, and in the midst
of the crowd you will praise God. This should make
you neither sad nor vain, for God has called you
precisely for this and he delights in his people. Hence
your mission to praise and intercede. Remember that
to pray in God's temple is to pray in communion with
the Church, in the unity of the body of Christ. But

16

Christ's body is made up of all believers; hence he who prays in the temple is heard, since he who prays in communion with the Church prays in spirit and in truth.[9]

Ps. 35:18; 149:4

Love the liturgy chosen by your community and be present punctually and faithfully. Be both docile and active, knowing that by this you are serving the church and doing what is pleasing to God. I shall make them rejoice in a house of prayer; their prayers and their offerings will be accepted on my altar, for my house will be called a house of prayer for all peoples.

Exod. 12:16
Ps. 22:23
Isa. 56:7

Love the church where the liturgy is performed and be full of respect, calm, serenity and recollection in this holy temple, so that your example and the mere sight of you may draw people to prayer and peace.

1 Thess. 4:12

As you don the liturgical cowl for the offices remind yourself that your baptism in Christ has truly clothed you with him and that you have become wholly a song of praise to his glory. Put on this robe and wear this habit in the twofold light of Christ covering you and the Spirit invading you. Be the body of Christ and the temple of the Spirit to the glory of the Father.

Gal. 3:27
Eph. 1:14
1 Cor. 6:19
Eph. 2:20–2

Daily Eucharist, finally, should be the climax of your continual prayer, where you reach the highest level of union with your brothers, each being a member of Christ's body like you, and with God who thus lives in you as you live in him.

1 Cor. 12:27
John 6:56

---

[9] St Augustine.

3 Work

23 Work.

Man works. The Christian works. The monk works. A threefold reason for you to work zealously.[1]

Delight and imitate your God by your work.

John 5:17 The Father works, creating, judging and upholding the world.

Mark. 6:3
Heb. 1:3 The Son works, by becoming a carpenter, sustaining the universe by his word.

The Spirit works untiringly, renewing the hearts of men and the face of the earth.

Be glad of living, by work, in the image of God.

Gen. 1:28;
3:19
1 Cor. 4:12 . To share in the achievement of creation, and to control the earth; to share in its redemption by earning your bread with the sweat of your brow as God commands, son of Adam, work hard with your own hands.

1 Cor. 10:31 By hard work, live the daily Passover from suffering to offering, from constraint to acceptance; and from being merely submissive, you will become a son sharing his Father's work. Thus unified, may you do all for God's glory.

Work will make you both fulfilled and purified, loyal to your fellow-man and close to your God.

24 Two good reasons oblige you to work:

On the one hand, to support the community by living on the work of your hands, so that neither you nor your brothers may be a burden to anyone; on the 2 Thess. 3:8 other hand, to assist the weak and help the needy.[2]

[1] St Basil, *Longer Rule* 37.
[2] ibid. 42.

So your work will be wholly guided by charity since what you earn will be for your brothers and the poor.

Do not cease working until evening.

Make a point of doing manual work. If you don't want to work, neither should you eat. Work quietly in the Lord Jesus and eat the bread you yourself have earned.

If you are poor you have to work in order to live, but you also work because you have a right to your keep. Your work should make you humble and free.

Acts 20:35
Eph. 4:28

Eccles. 11:6
1 Thess. 4:11
2 Thess. 3:10, 12

Ecclus. 31:4
Matt. 10:10

25   By working, you also show solidarity with the urban world and the mass of its workers, whether working or looking for work, whether happy at it or putting up with it.

For you it is the special place where you meet your fellow-men, exactly where they are; and a service you give at the heart of the city you are called to belong to. There are six days during which you should labour. And Jesus the man said as much, and acted accordingly.

Exod. 20:9;
35:1
Deut. 5:13
Luke 13:14
Mark 6:3

To be closer to other men and at the same time show your free dependence, you will not engage in private enterprise. You are to be a *wage-earner*, merely bearing in mind that the worker deserves his salary. This is precisely the way you will learn the meaning of dependence and humble submission. At the same time, how to receive with one hand and give away with the other, never closing your fist over your own earnings.

Luke 10:7
1 Tim. 6:18

By choosing to work as hard as possible, but not more than you ought, not primarily in view of a perishable end but one that lasts for ever, you are to stand free and challenging in a world where work has been overrated into a religion and often into a sacred cow, a world of confrontation and competition, of alienation and the rat-race for material wealth.

John 6:27–8

26   By doing *part-time* work and often accepting a minimum wage, you will remind the world more by

deed than by word, of the parallel values of prayer, generosity, silence, the brotherly life, peaceful hospitality and worship, and that we have always to seek first the Kingdom of God and his righteousness. For what use is it if a man gain the whole world and ruin his own life?

Matt. 6:33
Luke 9:25

Hence, consent humbly and clear-sightedly, to work only part-time, outside the house, keeping for contemplation, the common life, solitude, study, hospitality and rest, all the time needful for a peaceful, balanced life. Perhaps there, above all, Christ means you to find the prophetic dimension of your monastic life.

All this you will bear witness to, not by leaving the world but by staying in it without belonging to it. Humbly and bravely consent to live this way, without always being able to justify your choice nor even to account for it. Be willing to live it in all its imperfection and fragmentation, even perhaps to the point of feeling that you are going against your very self. But if you want to follow him, deny yourself, take up your cross each day and walk in his footsteps.

Matt. 16:24

To express the value of solitary contemplation to the worker's world, and to the contemplative world the worth of corporate labour, put your prayer into your work and your work into your prayer. Give work its true value in union with the divine worker, Jesus, the carpenter.[3]

The monks of old held that the duty of prayer could be fulfilled while they worked.[4] So according to the apostle you can pray without ceasing and at the same time work day and night.

1 Thess. 5:17
2 Thess. 3:8

27 In the morning, when men go out to work till evening, listen to the Lord's voice saying: Child, go and work in my vineyard.

Ps. 104:23
Matt. 21:28
Ps. 90:17

Murmur from morning to night: Prosper, Lord, the work of my hands.

As evening draws in, offer everything to the Father:

[3] Charles de Foucauld.
[4] St Basil, *Longer Rule* 37.

I am but a useless servant; I have done only what I ought.

Luke 17:10

Sweet then will be your workman's sleep and God will bless the fruit of your labour.

Eccles. 5:11
Deut. 14:29

The role of political commitment with all its cleavages, compromises and clashes, is not for you. Yours is to stand upright in justice and truth and to proclaim by your life the Gospel of peace. As an urban monk, the only politics you are committed to at the heart of the city is doing what God approves.

Eph. 6:15
Ps. 87:2

28   You may not choose your work on your own initiative. And you would be guilty of the sin of pride and of disobedience[5] if you refused the task imposed.

Depending on what is appropriate and what you are asked to do, be ready to work with equal joy inside or outside the monastery. Do not take pride in earning a lot, nor get bitter if you earn little, knowing that with your brothers, communally, praying, studying or working turn by turn, it is communally that we, with one heart and soul and in the same spirit, should work at God's work and, transcending all other, however necessary, tasks, together choose to live the better part. Everything matters, but God alone suffices.[6]

Phil. 2:2
John 6:29
Luke 10:42

You should, therefore, work out with the prior and the council, the work you may choose or accept and under what conditions.

In this matter trust the wisdom of the ancients and the Fathers when they say: The general principle is to choose those occupations which favour the peace and tranquillity of our lives, that are technically not too difficult and which do not require us to make harmful or undesirable contacts.[7]

---

[5] ibid. 41.
[6] St. Teresa of Avila.
[7] St Basil, *Longer Rule* 38.

29 If your work is to lead to personal integration and reveal its profound value and hidden mysticism, it should be:

† Useful: not a mere pastime or condescension or concession that would make it vain or optional;

† Well done: each must be carefully attentive to his own work, doing it under God's eye with active zeal and eager solicitude . . . not flitting futilely from one occupation to another;[8]

† Unprofitable: dependent both on employer and on community, working limited hours, playing fair with your fellow-workers, and handing back any gains immediately so as never to enrich yourself;

† Lived as witness through your seriousness, fidelity, willingness, joy, keenness, discretion and enthusiasm; faith without proselytism but never silent through shame;

2 Cor. 4:2

† Balanced and practical, respecting other commitments, your day in the desert, presence at the liturgy; demanding but never exhausting nor alienating;

Rom. 13:8
Gal. 5:14

† Above all it should be an opportunity for prayer and charity, since love is the bond of all perfection.

And before everything else, work out your salvation in fear and trembling; for God is there working in you, inspiring both the will and the deed for his own chosen purposes.

Phil. 2:12–13

Whatever you do, do it wholeheartedly as for the Lord.

Col. 3:23

---

[8] ibid.

4 Silence

30   Enter into the mystery of silence.

Your goal in life is not to hold your tongue but to love your brothers, to know yourself and to receive your God. You need to learn how to listen, how to retreat into the depths, how to rise above yourself.

Silence leads you to all this, so seek it lovingly and vigilantly.

But beware of false silence: yours should be neither taciturnity nor glumness, nor should it be systematic or inflexible, or torpid.

Authentic silence is the gateway to peace, adoration and love.

Live your silence, don't merely endure it. You will love it only if you learn its value and its cost. Theory will not be much help here. But, once experienced, you will be unable to do without it. Two motives can lead you to choose silence practised in seclusion for God's sake. Either you have already reached such a level of purity and knowledge that you experience God, or else you have heard someone speak of it as a good thing and relying on this you set out to acquire it.[1]

So pray for the grace of true silence; Mary has the secret. She treasured all her memories faithfully and pondered them in her heart.

If you love truth be a lover of silence. Like the sun it will enlighten you in God. It will liberate you from false knowledge and to you open this very silence of God.[2]

[1] Philoxenus of Mabbug.
[2] Isaac of Nineveh.

31 God is silence. His all-powerful Word came to us from his tranquil silence. And it was in the murmur of a gentle breeze that he revealed himself to the prophet. Your silence will lead you to listen to the supreme Word and in the centre of your heart you will hear a voice murmuring: Come to the Father.

Wisd.
18:14–15 Through him you will enter into the mystery of God and your heart will be opened to the joy of his pres-
' 1 Kings 19:12 ence and the grace of adoration.

Material silence will introduce you to spiritual silence and spiritual silence lead you to life with God. But if you cease to live in silence, communication with God will become impossible.[3]

Silence takes you to God and God leads you into his silence. He who does the will of God will never cease to hear his inner voice.

Therefore, let the Lord delve deep into your heart and create an expectancy and a call disposing you to receive and keep the Father's Word, who is his Son, in the peace of the Spirit. Taste this divine Word, uttered in total silence; trinitarian silence, fully attentive, respectful, sharing and loving. Only contemplation of this mystery will lead you in your turn to live the secret of inner silence; and in its peaceful and steadfast silence your life will manifest
John 1:8 God. Like John you will bear witness to the Light.

At work, in the street, coming and going, alone or by public transport, in the midst of the bustling city, bear about with you the secret of your inner silence. Each day keep wide spaces of silence, and when night comes, meditate on your bed in peace and silence. God lives in you, listen to him. Silence is the well-spring of your prayer at the heart of the city and the
Ps. 4:5 daily peace of your soul.

32 Among your brothers, with them and for them, live your silence.

Silence of the lips: by avoiding too much talk you will escape superficiality, backbiting, frivolity, and, by this same token, sin. The man who guards his

---

[3] Philoxenus of Mabbug.

24

words keeps his life, and the over-talkative man is lost. For abundance of words is not without fault. Beg God to set a muzzle on your mouth and to watch over the door of your lips. When faced with murmuring, gossip or banter, turn to prayer.

Prov. 13:3; 10:19
Ps. 141:3, 5

Go your way without letting your tongue stray and muzzle your mouth when wicked men talk in your presence.

Ps. 39:2

Silence of the heart: when false judgements, jealousy, unruly affections, nostalgia or memories burden or assault you. Humble yourself silently before God and he will raise you up.

Jas. 4:10

Resist the devil in this way and he will flee far from you; draw near to God and he will draw near to you. Learn this, brother, every thought not full of calm and humility is not according to God but is a so-called good inspiration coming from evil spirits. For our Lord comes with calm, but everything that is of the enemy is accompanied by turmoil and agitation.[4]

Jas. 4:8

33   *Silence of your whole being*: avoiding noise around you and keeping inward calm. You know that good makes no noise and noise does no good.[5] In the common life calm is necessary for the brothers who are praying, reading and writing, or at night, resting.[6] For love, then, watch your step, your work, your greetings and your speech. Silence too is charity.

Be discreet in the way you receive visitors, brief at the phone, concise in letter-writing, watchful over your tone of voice and measured in your laughter.[7]

On a deeper level *silence should teach you how to love*. It is the road to brotherly communion as well as its fruit. By it you will learn how to agree with your brothers and find a satisfactory balance between a life henceforth hidden with Christ in God, yet shared as the first way of expressing your mutual love.

Col. 3:3
Rom. 13:8

[4] Barsanuphius.
[5] St Francis of Sales.
[6] *Rule of Taizé*.
[7] St Basil, *Longer Rule* 17; St Benedict, *Rule* 7:10.

34   As St Benedict commands, never try to defend or protect a brother.[8] For in vain and useless words, you seriously risk losing what silence and prayer might have afforded you to help him come to his senses and make progress. Murmuring kills the community. Avoid it utterly.

Heb. 12:15
2 Tim. 2:23–6

You should not, however, remain speechless and mute in face of every wrong-doing or omission. At the right moment you should reprove, warn or exhort but always with patience and the desire to instruct. Both scripture and the Fathers say, one must be ready to speak out when a brother falls into error or sin.[9] Fair and honest brotherly correction does not disturb silence but leads to it, provided all is done in love.

2 Tim. 4:2
Lev. 19:17

Much better to complain than to nurse a grudge, and confession saves a man from disgrace. When necessary, then, first compose your differences by speaking to your brother and then come back and pray silently before the altar, and be capable of speaking out when brotherly correction requires it.

Ecclus. 20:2–3
Matt. 5:24

35   Sometimes the way to true charitable silence has to begin with words:

> Question your friend, he may have done nothing at all.
> And if he has done anything, he will not do it again.
> Question your neighbour; he may have said nothing at all.
> And if he has said anything, he will not say it again.
> Question your brother, for slander is very common.
> Do not believe all you hear.
> A man may make a slip without meaning what he says.
> And which of us has never sinned by speech?

Ecclus. 19:13–16

Live in trustful silence without suspicious thoughts or inner murmuring.

And then, be moderate. A wise man knows how to

---

[8] St Benedict, *Rule* 69.
[9] St Basil, *Shorter Rule* 47.

keep silence till the right moment. Speak if need be,
but briefly, be concise and ready both to be listened
to and to be silent.

Prov. 11:12
Ecclus. 32:7

The more words one uses the greater is the emp-
tiness of it all; and where is the advantage in that?

Eccles. 6:11

36   Silence will teach you to build up *the inner man*
who must each day be renewed in the image of his
Creator.

Col. 3:10

When you are troubled, tempted or tired, silence
will set things right. It will teach you self-control,
restraint, self-mastery, for scripture says if you do not
sin by the tongue you are a perfect man and able to
control your whole body.

James 3:2

Silence will help you lose bad habits, cleanse you
from inward chatter and help you to find right attitudes and sincere words.

Prov. 10:19

So long as you have not forgotten worldly ways and
talk, you will find it impossible to discern the tone of
voice, discretion in speech, the opportune moment,
the special nature of terms familiar and particular to
those who live prayerful lives. But silence enables you
to forget old habits by letting them drop and gives
you time to learn good ones. Hence, as far as you can,
be silent.[10]

37   In the crucible of silence you will learn holiness,
since silence is the door to humility, contemplation
and mercy. By leading you to self-forgetfulness,
silence will allow you to discover God and in the heart
of God you will rediscover the world by God's light.

So live outward silence and enjoy it inwardly and
you will taste the perfect delight of those who keep
his commandments in their hearts and dwell silently
in his love.

John 15:10-11

With your community settle times and places where
you will be required to keep silence or allowed to
exchange a few words, to relax or be quiet, and respect

[10] ibid. 13.

these times and places. Then silence will be bound up with obedience and humility.

Eccles. 3:4
1 Cor. 13:16 When the time comes *to share or relax* (for example, on Sunday evenings), join in gaily, for there is a time for laughter, and love delights in the truth.

38 Be very careful about your weekly *day in the desert* and live it according to Christ's example, for he loved to withdraw in this way and encouraged his disciples to do likewise. Nothing should deprive you of this day for, as an urban monk, you need it for your physical, psychological and spiritual balance. At the heart of these solitary days God is calling you to draw Matt. 14:13
Luke 9:18
Hos. 2:16 you to himself, to lead you into the desert and there, silently, speak to your heart.

Lastly, look on the *great silence* of each evening with St Benedict and the Fathers[11] as a singular blessing. For night is an immense mystery, bearer of the secret of creation, incarnation, resurrection and the return that will come at the dead of night. In this nocturnal Luke 12:35–8
Matt. 25:6
Luke 21:36
Ps. 134:2; 17:3
Isa. 26:9
S. of S. 5:2 silence, watch and pray. God visits your heart in the night. Do you, then, bless the Lord in the darkness. Desire him in the night with your whole soul and let your spirit seek God in silence, within. You sleep in peace, brother, but your heart watches.

Ps. 51:17 At dawn the Lord himself will open your lips and your mouth will cry out his praise.

And so you stand ready to welcome the grace of a new day.

---

[11] St Benedict, *Rule* 42.

5 Hospitality

39   Be hospitable and share.

God became man so that in man you might discover God. When you welcome men you meet God.

Whoever receives a man, in fact, receives Christ and whoever receives him in that very way receives the One who sent him.   *Matt. 10:40–2 / Mark 9:37*

By this very fact he actually meets the Father whom no man has ever seen. In a wonderful way hospitality and sharing lead you to contemplate God.   *John 1:18*

Since God is also himself hospitality and sharing, by following this rule you act like him and are led in a wonderful way to imitate him.

That is why hospitality has always been held to be a typical monastic virtue. Silence, fervour, penitence and solitude are not enough. Only love is the supreme good.

Ask the Lord to make you grasp this mystery.

In your heart God has excavated an immense space where he has placed a precious treasure. From now on you have the twofold duty of receiving and giving: sharing the treasure of the kingdom you bear within you and stretching the area of your tent for those around you.   *2 Cor. 4:7 / Matt. 6:19–20 / Isa.54:2*

40   Welcome God.

Unless you are God-filled there will be no sharing and giving; unless he lives in you, you will be unable to welcome people sincerely. If through prayer and love you open your heart to the presence of God it will radiate from you. God's graces are given only to be shared.   *Luke 18:17*

Since you have nothing you have not received, keep

nothing you cannot give away. Welcome God in order
to share him.

Be welcoming towards your community.

Welcome one another, says the apostle, as Christ
welcomed us, for the glory of God. There is no future
for a divided household and only a united Fraternity
is capable of giving hospitality.

Each day and every instant of the day open your
inmost heart to your brothers. Love them just as they
are and not as you would wish them to be. What is
the use of endless outside contacts, if at home there is
no real acceptance of one another? Be humble always,
gentle and patient. Be forbearing with one another
and charitable. Open-heartedness in community will
teach you how far you may open your doors to the
outside world.

1 Cor. 4:7

Rom. 15:7
Matt. 12:25

Eph. 4:2–3

41   Welcome your fellow-men.

Remember to show hospitality. There are some who
by so doing have entertained angels without knowing
it.

Welcome the *city*. By choosing to live there, you
welcome its rhythms, laws, problems, tragedies,
difficulties and holiness. Bound up like this with its
life, your life-style and faith should make you credible
in its eyes. As silver is smelted in a crucible, so will
you be smelted in the heart of the city, like Christ in
Jerusalem.

Welcome *its citizens*. These are the people who
surround you, whom you rub shoulders with and
entertain. They pray with you, thirsty for living water,
tormented with fatigue, anxiety, solitude, anonymity
and noise. For their sake, try to create an oasis of
prayer and peace.

Welcome *your district*, just as it is, and remember
you live there under the twofold obligation of good
neighbourliness and witness. Never be a cause of
stumbling or the derision and contempt of those
around you.

Heb. 13:2

Ezek. 22:22
Luke 13:33

Matt. 18:5–7
Ps. 44:14

42   *Guests* who come to the door must be received like Christ. As you hurry to meet them, full of charitable thoughtfulness, humbly greet their arrival and departure, in order to honour Christ in them,[1] recalling the precious tradition of monastic hospitality.

Welcome your *relatives* and those of your brothers with cordial joy. Remember God commands you to honour and serve them as the Lord. Besides, since they no longer have the joy of welcoming you often at home, they should always be able to count on receiving a warm welcome from you.

Exod. 20:12
Ecclus. 3:6–8
Tobit 4;3

Pay special attention to those who live on the fringes of modern society, or are its *outcasts*, those whom Jesus called the sick, the prisoners and the foreigners . . . For you, they are a special presence of Christ. Let them share your meals, your hope, your faith. When an alien settles on your land you are not to oppress him; he is to be treated as a native born among you and you are to love him as yourself.

Matt.
25:31–46
Lev. 19:33

43   Welcome those who will always be the *poor* among us. For, alas, the poor will always be with you in this land and for that reason I command you to be open-handed with your countrymen, with the poor and the distressed in your own land. When one of your countrymen in any of the settlements which the Lord your God gives you becomes poor, do not be hard-hearted or close-fisted with him in his need. Be open-handed towards him and lend him what he needs. And when you give, give freely and do not begrudge him your bounty.

Luke
14:12–14
Deut. 15:11,
7, 10

Welcome each one without prejudice or shrinking, remembering Christ, the man, who welcomed sinners and ate with them. For many people, monastic life in urban conglomerations can be a quiet and persuasive call to conversion. In this matter, put no obstacles in the way of God's grace.

Luke 15:2

Finally, welcome *children*. Give them a special place in the liturgy and imitate Christ who welcomed them and ordered them to be allowed to approach him, and

[1] St Benedict, *Rule* 53.

even wished to be seen in a unique way through them.
Luke 9:48   Let the children come to me, do not stop them, for
Mark 10:14   the kingdom of heaven belongs to such as these.

44   Silently and open-handedly, welcome the guests
that providence sends to your table. Besides a meal,
you offer them a space of calm and peace and your
prayer can only be nourished by these contacts. Think
of all that Jesus did, said and revealed while at meals
and of his promise that his followers should all eat
and drink one day at his table in his kingdom. In this
Matt. 9:10;   broken world, God sees the table as a sacred thing. A
26:7, 17; 19:28   forgotten treasure for you to rediscover and cherish.
The Fraternity itself should look hospitable. It
should be kept clean, and greetings should be gay and
spontaneous. In the church there should be the feeling
of a presence and the evocation of a mystery; all necessary information should be given in clear and precise
terms. Those called upon to be receptionists should
be especially obliging, pleasant and attentive, but
discreet.[2]

45   But however wholehearted and generous your
hospitality, it also needs to be given with discernment.
Be humbly aware of your limitations. Keep up your
hospitality but never let the Fraternity degenerate into
an information or social service bureau. Conserve your
energy, your silence, prayer and time. Know how to
cut a conversation short, to put off a visit, to go
straight to the point. Thoughtful listening does not
mean lengthy conversations. It is not a good thing to
2 Tim. 2:16   let yourself go, and so run the risk of being swept
Eph. 4:14   away by every wind of doctrine, like children, carried
2 Tim. 4:3   off your feet by futile discourse.
Clearly, you cannot possibly have an answer to
every question nor meet all demands. So try and teach
your relatives and friends to grasp the new obligations
Luke 14:26   of your state of life. If your ideal is genuine they will

[2] St Basil, *Longer Rule* 32.

understand. Christ has called you to separate yourself from all you hold dear.

Matt. 19:29
Luke 14:25–7

46   Be wideawake to the *dangers* of unlimited hospitality and lack of communal discernment. You might reach saturation point and end by becoming superficial, distracted or monopolized. Do not be nowhere in your effort to be everywhere, or attentive to no one simply because you are running after everyone. Availability and spontaneity in prayer in the name of all would be hindered if you let yourself be held captive by a small group. In the heart of God you live in all men's hearts.

    Never monopolize a guest. Do not let hospitality become a distraction and, as St Basil advises, do not lose your way in it, but rather let those with the charism of the Word, and who know how to speak and listen with such wisdom as builds up faith, be the ones to receive visitors.[3] Let your conversation be always gracious and never insipid; study how best to talk with each person you meet, far from any kind of superficiality, trivial talk or idle chatter.

Col. 4:6

47   As soon as you enter monastic life, make clear-cut *breaks*; launch out into the deep. Leave your address book behind and hang up your telephone. Find your parents, relatives and friends first in God. Believe deeply in the communion of saints. God is stronger than your strength and if you forsake everything for him you will receive a hundredfold already in this life, and in the heart of God you will receive all the real treasures of eternal life and share them with everyone.

Matt. 19:27–9

    Hold on at all costs to that most precious afternoon space for spiritual reading. In city life it is both vital and essential. Receive no visits at that time.

    Make no outside calls without first consulting the prior to make sure whether they will be useful, or whether it would be better to postpone them.

[3] cf. ibid. 66; St Basil, *Shorter Rule* 32.

48   Although you are not enclosed, you will gradually discover the amount of *enclosure* you and your brothers need: places and times in and during which nothing and no one may distract, monopolize or disturb you. There you will learn the blessed secret of restraining your words, thoughts and heart so as to build up and sustain your inner self.

Strong in love and detachment you are now ready to share in the most precious of all God's gifts: the table of his Word and of his Eucharist. The very essence of your hospitality lies precisely in this: *to receive in prayer, through prayer and for prayer*. Opening up a source is more important than busying yourself with structures. Dig the well, then, and share the

John 7:38   living water promised to those who believe in him.

49   Ultimately, it is probably more important to try *to be welcome* than to *welcome*. Welcomed for what you are.

Be your genuine self. Then people will know you as you really are.

Be perfect like your heavenly Father and you will

Matt. 5:48   bear witness to the One who makes you holy.

Be blameless and pure, children of God without stain in the midst of a world where you will shine with your brothers as a source of light. Fearlessly and noiselessly, let your life point the way to the source, and God himself will welcome and appease the weary.

Phil. 2:15   Saints do not need to be heard; their very existence
Jer. 31:25   is a call. And God's wisdom speaks through their lips.

Come, eat my bread and drink my wine prepared

Prov. 9:1–6   for you. In the end it is God himself who welcomes,
John 6:45–58   nourishes, serves and teaches all of us.

MONASTIC

6 Monks and Nuns

50   The vocation of the brothers and sisters of Jerusalem is *monastic*.

Our primary aim lies not in creating an apostolic, priestly or charitable community life but in desiring deeply and wholeheartedly to become nuns and monks together.

Monastic life is not something to be conquered but a place where you are brought to birth. Though the Spirit, making all things new, urges you to live your life freely, you may not ignore the immense wealth of reflection, experience, wisdom and sanctity lived and transmitted by all those around us or by our predecessors. In its main features your route is already mapped out and the Church calls on you to follow it.

Listen, my son, to the precepts of the Master, lend the ear of your heart, gladly welcome the teaching of the Father who loves you and put it perfectly into practice.[1] I am the Lord your God. I teach you for your own advantage and lead you along the way you must go.   Isa. 48:17

51   Do not imagine, then, that by trying at all costs to innovate or improvise, you will go faster or better. Better to limp along the right road than to take great strides off the track. For even if he doesn't make much headway, a man who hobbles along the right road gets nearer to the goal, whereas the one who is off the track gets further from the goal the more energetically he runs.[2] So be convinced that you are upheld by the prayer of all your ancestors as you

[1] St Benedict, *Rule*, prologue.
[2] St Thomas Aquinas.

tread this monastic route and that you learn from the experience of the Fathers.

Today God wants us to carry on the tradition of all these holy lives, in spite of our imperfections, surrounded as we are by such a cloud of witnesses.

Heb. 12:1

The Spirit and the Church (scripture and tradition) teach us the meaning of the monastic vocation.

52 The monastic life is first of all *evangelical*.

It is the direct expression of our baptismal charism by which we pass with Christ from death to life, so that we too may live a new life. The monk is simply a complete Christian. His striving is for a radical living of the Gospel in a total prophetic gesture. So as to be central to the Christian plan, he is ready to be the field where grace can bring forth the new creation of man by God and the deification of man in God.

Rom. 6:4

The monastic mystery is nothing other than the unique essence of the Gospel, that is to say, the acceptance of everything being ordered and subordinated to the living, loving and fulfilling meeting with God. Directed towards the reconquest of this image and this likeness, the entire monastic life is a process of deification, leading towards the likeness of one same, ever more glorious, image, that of the only Son himself.

Luke 10:42
Gen. 1:26
Eph. 4:13

Your baptism has set an infinite desire for God germinating within, and this makes your soul vibrate to a continual call to sanctity. Responding to your monastic vocation, answer this baptismal call. To the Word of divine love, respond with the word of your Christian faith, of faith manifesting itself in charity. You will be a true monk or nun if you are one of the baptized who loves, prays, works, shares and rests in God; if, in the spirit of the beatitudes, you seek nothing in this world but God alone, the uniquely necessary. Get to the roots of the Gospel: there, spelt out, is the whole secret of the monastic life.

Gal. 5:6

53   The monastic life, centred on and directed towards God, is *theocentric*.

Before all else, the monk's life is a search for God. His very existence is unceasingly turned to the day when he will meet him. What better aim in life than this luminous goal? The monk and nun make a point of never forgetting this. Tending towards this promised end, they are fired with the hope of the watchman awaiting certain dawn, and borne on the love of the faithful fiancée, lamp aglow, expecting the return of her beloved. God made you for himself and your heart will never rest till it rests in him.[3] When you enter the monastery be careful to see if you are really seeking God,[4] or if perhaps you are not looking for some emotional prop, an apostolate or even a spiritual atmosphere, and not first and foremost God himself. If this is truly your aim then set off to the place and day of meeting, not content to wait passively but responding wholeheartedly to God's authentic call. For the kingdom of heaven suffers violence, and the violent are the ones to capture it first, at the cost of greatest renunciation.

Ps. 130:6
Matt. 25:6–7;
11:12
Luke 16:16

54   The monastic life is being *present to God*.

We are immersed in a mystery: before, behind and in us there is someone. God *is*. He is *there* and he speaks. He speaks to you and you live under his eye. The monk strives to live in the presence of this unique person who is both the *Thou* to whom all his love is addressed, and the *I* who initially addresses him from pure love. God has called you by name and you make bold to call him by his. You know your name is engraved on his divine hands and you let the Lord impress his divine name on your forehead and fasten *his* law to your very hand. For the monk, everything, always and everywhere, is invested with the mystery of this omnipresence, transfiguring all he does, thinks and says. For the monk everything is a gift. God's icon is everywhere. Nothing and no one may be

---

[3] St Augustine.
[4] St Benedict, *Rule* 58.

preferred above this love. Nothing is profane, all is sacred—not sacralized but consecrated. The tiniest object, each fraction of a second, every happening leads to this presence and draws the monk to deep recollection. Contacts and meetings are all transformed. Lit with this light, transparent to this radiance, all day long everything becomes blessed with blessings, and time and space again becomes sacred; each element that goes to make up your life is in some way dissolved, re-fused and reconstructed to be reunified in God's fire. If you are a monk, God is everything for you. So you scarcely need to speak; your presence is the witness to whom God repeats: Walk before me. Like David or John the Baptist you stand face to face with God and go forward moved by this all-embracing summons. From now on your life is guided by this listening and you need not be concerned about clothes or food or the morrow, but only with the kingdom of God, which is within you.

Rev. 4:2
Isa. 49:16
Rev. 14:1
Deut. 6:8;
10:12; 26:17
1 Kings 3:6
Luke 1:17
Matt. 6:25–34

55   This presence of God entails being really *present to oneself*. The man in whom God dwells is dwelt in by himself. Prayer and silence draw him into his own deepest depths where he finds both himself and God. And in those depths there are no casual comings and goings. He lives as though enclosed: in the sense that he is a new being, fully alive with a fullness of the spirit; not a closed-up man but a man fully inhabited. When anyone is united to Christ he is a new creature; his old life is over, a new life has already begun and all comes from God.

Gal. 6:15
Eph. 3:16, 19
2 Cor. 5:17

You should not let this presence make you insensitive, distant or overbearing. On the contrary, it goes hand in hand with a fresh kind of attention to others and the world around you; a spiritual attention, thoughtful and loving, realistic and respectful. As you rediscover peace, your soul will be plunged into an almost paradisal joy, where everything—nature, objects, persons, events and all the ups and downs of life—is gradually transfigured in the light of this presence and this original memory rediscovered,

Ps. 41:13;

reminding us we have been made in his image and are destined one day to live in his presence for all eternity.

55:14; 140:14
Hos, 6:2

56   Like Abraham, walk in his presence and be perfect, and you will see and taste the goodness of the Lord whose joy it is to be your refuge.

Gen. 17:1

Watch yourself very carefully and hold yourself continually in God's presence so as not to do even the smallest thing contrary to his will. But whatever you want to do—speak, go and pay someone a visit, work, eat, drink or sleep—first see if it is what God wants; then you will be able to praise God as you do it; otherwise, desist. Thus, henceforth, you will act as you should in God's sight and you will praise him in all your thoughts and acts, and so draw very near him with great confidence.[5]

Aim at living *perpetually mindful of God* in the light of his presence with a burning desire to meet him, gladly giving up anything that could separate you from him so that you can repeat: I kept God in mind and was filled with joy.

Jonah 2:8
Tobit 4:5

The monk or nun is a person for whom God is enough.

57   The monastic life is an imitation of Christ and a walking in his footsteps: it is *christological*.

Since Jesus is the perfect image of man for God and of God for man, God passionately in love with man in a Man passionately in love with God, you are called to imitate the God-made-Man by uniting man and God in yourself. This *face* contains the sum of your monastic ideal.

You have heard the same call as St Antony, father of monks: if anyone wants to be my disciple, let him deny himself, take up his cross and follow me. If you love him, you must also follow and imitate him. That is your call: Christ suffered for you, leaving you a model, so that you could walk in his footsteps.

Matt. 16:24
1 Pet. 2:21

Your monastic life is living the mystery of the *Body*

[5] Abba Isaiah, *Apophthegmata*.

of Christ and the wedding of the Lamb, so as to be one only with him. If the Father is to love you, be like his only Son, identified with him so completely that you can say, The life I live now is not my life but the life that Christ lives in me. One day the unification produced by monastic life should make you cry out, He dwells in me and I in him. For you, too, to live is Christ.

Gal. 2:20
John 6:56
Phil. 1:21

58   A monk's life is full when he manages to give himself up to the *fullness of being God's son.* Since he no longer seeks earthly food he becomes that much the more the son of the heavenly Father who lives in and feeds him. Since he refuses to follow Mammon, better to serve peace, he becomes that much the more the son of God. And since he refuses to come to terms with sin he is made perfect as the heavenly Father is perfect. By withdrawing his gaze from earth, he allows himself to be drawn up with the Son of God reascending to the heights. Instead of this passing world, the home he looks for is in heaven where the Son has gone to prepare a place for him. Seeking God and God only, in Christ he finds the radiant fullness of the Godhead who has come to meet his human nature in the flesh to transfigure it. Ravished with joy, he has discovered a spring within him murmuring, *Come to the Father.* A voice tells him, I am ascending now to my Father and your Father, towards my God and your God, and the monk takes the same road.

Matt. 6:32;
5:9, 48
Eph. 4:8
Heb. 11:16
John 14:3
Phil. 3:20–1
John 20:17

59   This is what *imitation of Christ* commits you to in the monastic ideal. Imitation will lead to identification, identification to incorporation and incorporation to divinization. If you have forsaken everything, you will share everything in the Father's heart. For where his Son is, there he wants you to be with him, to contemplate his glory.

John 17:24

There is one single name that crystallizes this incredible adventure: the name above all names, the Name, privileged meeting-place of God and man, the

Name endowed with all the agility and power of the Spirit; revealed to Mary who with Joseph was the first to hear it and was the first to murmur it to him; the Name that should gradually absorb you and by which you will be so absorbed that a lifetime will not suffice to learn it, say it and pray it, the Name by which you are already saved, inscribed in letters of love, blood and fire: the Name of *Jesus*. This is the Name that purifies, liberates, simplifies, unifies and creates the monk in the breath of the Spirit. Let your whole monastic life be nothing but a living of the name of Jesus.

Phil. 2:9
Matt. 1:21
Luke 1:31
Phil. 2:10

60   The monastic vocation is *spiritual*. Those who live it are to be bearers of light and the Spirit. Their essential task is to let the spiritual beauty of the creation transfigured by the Holy Spirit shine forth through them.

The soul that possesses wisdom bears in itself a kind of splendour of eternal light and a reflection of God's majesty, and just as it is inwardly penetrated with God's grace, so outwardly it diffuses an emanation of the splendour and love of God . . . Thus do God's friends receive already here below something of the glorification they will obtain fully there above.[6]

61   Let the original image of God rise up from the ground of your being and he will make you into a final Likeness, as befits the action of the Lord who is the Spirit. If you let him live and act in you, on you this Spirit will gradually bestow an immense freedom above all laws and institutions. Subject to all, you will be free of all, possessed by the Word of God, and henceforth proclaiming it, in silence, a whole life of love.

2 Cor. 3:15–18
Gal. 5:25
1 Cor. 9:19

The monk prays unceasingly to God so as to purify his spirit from a host of conflicting thoughts and so that his spirit may become a monk within him, alone before the true God, shutting out evil thoughts, at all

[6] William of St-Thierry.

times pure and intact before God.[7] Since the Spirit is
our life, may the Spirit move us so to act that, whether
we wake or sleep, we may live united with Christ.

Gal. 5:25
1 Thess. 5:10

62   In this sense the monastic life is also called
angelic: neither disincarnate nor uncommitted but
turned frankly towards heaven where God lives. All
Christians are caught up in this ascending movement;
all of us are in some way already in heaven, and it
would be illusory to live as if our future were in this
world. With Jesus we have been raised by the Father
to sit in the heavens with Christ. Your monastic
vocation, then, urges you to seek the things that are
above, where Christ is, to think of the things of
heaven, not those of earth—for you are already dead
and your life is henceforth hidden with Christ in God.
There, where true joys are to be found. That the
heavenly and invisible things are the most immediate
and real, you will not grasp at the outset: visible things
only last for a while, the invisible ones are eternal.
This is precisely the opposite to the glory sought by
the world. One day we shall all be like angels in
heaven.

Eph. 2:6
Col. 3:1–3
2 Cor. 4:18
John 5:44
Mark 12:25

With a pure heart and changed mind, strive for that
unclouded vision by which you are able to see God;[8]
and in the liturgy sing to the Lord in communion
with the angels and saints. By entering the monastic
life you drew near Mount Sion, the city of the living
God, the heavenly Jerusalem, the myriads of angels,
the assembly of the first-born whose names are written
in heaven. Happy is he whose heart is pure: he will
see God with the angels.

Heb. 12:22–23
Matt. 5:8;
18:10

63   Because of this the monastic vocation is also
prophetic.
In every aspect of their life, the monk and nun
remind the world of the temporary character of
present day conditions, and the institutional church

[7] St Macarius, *Homily* 56.
[8] St Bruno.

44

that their unique aim, transcending liturgy, legalism and morality, is always this total and immediate communion with God. Truly I see you live a prophetic life. For to walk in the Spirit, to live by faith, to seek what is above and not what is on earth, to forget what is behind and to reach out to what is to come; this is truly to prophesy. A partial prophecy as yet, but no less great.[9]

Be at the heart of the world as a fire kindled by Christ to remind it of his burning demands, and as a prophet of the second coming remind the world of this vibrant hope. Walk in the footsteps of Elias and John the Baptist, the outstanding models of all monastic life. Consecrated in the Spirit, the monk is called to interpret the visible and scrutinize the invisible, to turn the here-and-now Godwards and to proclaim what is to come in the light of his faith. Do not be afraid of always going straight to the heart of things and, if necessary, of living at cross purposes with the world. Suffering will come, but take courage, Christ has overcome the world. Search out God's footsteps in daily life, seek his face in the unseen, fix your eye on the reward and, as though you saw the invisible prize, stand firm.

Luke 12:49
John 16:33
Heb. 11:26-7

64   All this will lead you to grasp the *eschatological* nature of your calling.

Monastic labour is one long anticipation of the coming of the kingdom of God and even now a foretaste of what is promised here above.

The monk is someone to whom God has spoken, whom God has taken to himself and who has allowed himself to be taken. From now on he burns with intense desire to see God and enter into an ever-increasing and never-ending dialogue with him. Like Jacob wrestling with God the whole night long, he goes on repeating, I will not let you go till you bless me. The monk and nun are driven on by this irresistible attraction to be at last with God alone, the better to serve and rediscover in him what they forsook for

[9] St Bernard, *Sermon* 37:6.

45

his sake. So they are led to do everything possible to reach this point in their outward observances and inward purifications. The reason they love God is God himself, and the measure of their love is to love him without measure.[10]

Jer. 20:7
John 14:8
Gen. 32:27

65 They know God is ever the pure, inaccessible Being, totally Other and the most Holy. To reach him on their own is beyond their power and, were they to see him, they would die. And that is exactly what they want, to *die*. Not to life but to their old nature, the world, sin and all those obstacles that prevent their seeing, living and growing. They realize that, if to climb to God is impossible, they can receive him into their hearts and find him in its depths. Following Jesus, they see a new road opening up before them and with him they are drawn towards heaven. For you died, as it is written, and now your life lies hidden with Christ in God. In union with Christ Jesus, the Father has raised us up and enthroned us with him in the heavenly realms. Once they have seen a small door opened in the heavens and a narrow road leading to life, their whole objective is to set out along this way, passing through this door to plunge forthwith into the vision of the invisible.

2 Sam. 22:27
Isa. 6:3
Exod. 33:22–5
1 John 3:2
John 14:23
1 John 4:13
John 10:9;
14:6
Col. 3:3
Eph. 2:6
Matt. 7:14
John 1:51; 3:7

Eyes fixed on this happy end, may your monastic life be from now on *the dawn of your eternity*.

Heb. 11:26

66 Think, then, of yourself as an exile, traveller and stranger on earth, aspiring to a better, heavenly land. Imagine yourself as living the last day of your life, and in the light of this examine your daily life, as if this day were indeed your last. This is why monks have always liked to meditate on death and the last things. If you are to live by anticipation in heaven,[11] do not wait for your death in order to die! Forget the distance already covered and go straight ahead, running with all your might for the prize God calls

Heb. 11:13,16

[10] St Bernard.
[11] Elizabeth of the Trinity.

you to receive on high in Christ Jesus. There the Lord
has prepared for you eternal glory out of all measure.

Phil. 3:14
2 Cor. 4:17

67   There is no reaching this state unless you truly die
to yourself. Mystical the monastic life may be, but it
remains basically *ascetic*.

Renunciation comes first.

Without it there is no being Christ's disciple.
Unhesitating and unlimited renunciation is needed
more in a monastic than an apostolic vocation. The
true monk forsakes everything at once and for ever,
to save his life by losing it for God. To be absorbed
in the world to come you must have left this passing
world. You cannot serve two masters. The measure-
ment of your attachment to God's will is the measure-
ment of your detachment from this world; in this let
God measure for you. Do not measure your renunciations, and the joy of measureless love will be yours.
You will already possess the happiness of the hundredfold promised to those who have forsaken everything
already in this life.

Luke 9:23f;
14:25f
Matt. 6:24
Mark 4:24
John 16:22
Mark 10:30

68   Monasticism also calls for self-destitution.

The door of the kingdom is so narrow, it can only
be passed through naked. Like Christ, you will die
utterly destitute; and as monk and nun, you have
chosen freely to anticipate the day. Earthly goods are
blessed by God no doubt, but you have chosen to
distance yourself from them. The family is something
good but you consent to forsake it, to tear yourself
away from that which brought you into this world and
not to found that by which you yourself might bring
others into it. You will go even further, stripping
yourself of your own individuality to the point of
hating your own life, which is to perform the most
radical of all breaks with the past. What makes a
monk is this forsaking of any kind of personal project.
By calling you to be a monk or nun, Christ has
crucified the world for you and crucified you for the
world. And so, death works in you and life in him.

Job 1:21
1 Cor. 7:8, 32,
34
Luke 14:26
Ps. 40:9
Matt. 7:21
John 12:49–50
Gal. 6:14
2 Cor. 4:12

47

69   Hence, your monastic calling is to a life of joyous penitence and free privation.

Privation of food, by choosing (with common sense and no exaggeration) daily frugality and occasional fasts.

Privation of comfort, preferring need to ease because to take things easy is to stray from true peace.

Privation of sleep, by being content with a reasonable amount, from time to time watching at least one hour with Christ.

Mark 14:37

Many people will fail to understand all this. But you will live it in union with the One who suffered so much for you, completing in your body what is lacking to his Passion, and out of pity for the world of the poorest and for his Body the Church. When you renounce, strip and deprive yourself, consenting to lose everything to gain Christ, you are opening yourself to true life and perfect joy. This is the song of monastic life.

Col. 1:24
Phil. 3:8

70   This is why your vocation leads you actually to desire to leave this world. Not from disdain for this life or out of contempt for a world so deserving of love, but from a burning desire to anticipate the future life and enter a new existence as quickly as possible. Or do you not realize that baptism into union with Christ Jesus means baptism into his death? You have thus been buried with him through baptism, in death, so that, as Christ has been raised from death to the glory of the Father, you too may live a new life. Because he knows he cannot enter heaven without dying, the Christian makes sense, by his faith, of the senselessness of death caused by sin. To hasten this Passover, the monk chooses to die daily. No one takes his life from him but he gives it up freely. If he does not die he will remain alone, but if he dies here below he will already bear fruit here below. To be truly alive, monks and nuns freely choose to die! That the cross of Christ may not be in vain, they go to meet death as Christ did, in loving obedience to the Father of all love.

Eph. 4:22–3
Rom. 6:3–4;
5:12
1 Cor. 15:31
John 10:18;
12:24
1 Cor. 1:17
John 12:27
Heb. 5:8

48

> Whoever loves his life will lose it and whoever dies
> to his life in this world will keep it to all eternity.   John 12:25

71   Christ died for you, leaving an example for you
to follow in his footsteps. You need know nothing
else but Jesus Christ and Jesus Christ crucified. Your
monastic life must pass *by way of the cross*, not out of
desperation but for the sake of greater love. Die to
the world in order to open out to Life! Die to the
snare of evil, to enter into freedom! Die to yourself,
to be born anew! Die to death, the last and supreme
enemy of man and God, conquered by the Man-God,   1 Pet. 2:21
and you too will become incarnate with the power of   1 Cor. 2:2
the Godhead! At the heart of this sacrifice there opens   John 15:13
the road to your supreme freedom; it was so that you   1 Cor. 15:26,
might be free, that Christ nailed you with himself to   55
the cross and set you free.   Col. 2:9
     Gal. 5:1

72   To express this ideal of integral Christianity,
living its baptismal grace to the utmost limit, tradition
has coined a single, all-embracing word: MONASTIC.

It signifies a state in which you are both *one* and
alone.

The monk is alone (*monos*), One, unified, unique,
united to the unique and threefold God.[12] You are
called to follow Christ who was more and more alone
before his Father, as you too are alone before the
Alone.[13] You aim at seeking God in all things, always
and everywhere, in solitude or sharing, brotherly love
or deepest recollection, far from men or in the midst
of the world; your one desire, to meet the Father.
Hence, your need for silence and solitude. Your life
will be monastic if that is its atmosphere.   John 16:32

A monk's name comes first from the fact that he is
alone because he has renounced the world, within and
without . . . and because he clings to a totally Unique
One, that is, at every moment he rests his thought on
God alone.[14]

[12] Dionysius the Areopagite.
[13] Plotinus.
[14] St Macarius of Egypt.

49

73   Your essential closeness to God is expressed in a very precise and concrete way in your *cell*. For you, this should be a privileged time and the cell is the place you retire to and emerge from day by day. For it is there, in total privacy, that you will listen and pray best to your Father who sees you in secret, and stay in deep communion with the world, interceding for it in your prayer and preparing yourself to serve it better in your work, meetings, liturgy. Remember the teachings of the Fathers: sit in your cell and it

Matt. 6:6   will teach you all you need to know.[15]

74   The monk is also one (*unus*). Unified to be unifying, unified in himself and united with his brethren, and a bond of unity between earth and heaven, between man and God. Of itself, solitude has no special value, but only as a way to communion. This is why the monk is not only *monos* but also *unus*. Just as it is not good for a man to be alone, so the monk and nun aim, not at being solitary but at becoming beings of total communion. If the monk chooses to live somewhat apart from the world, this is because sin has confused and created divisions everywhere. He works step by step to build up unity

Gen. 2:18   and to let grace recreate unity in himself.

First then be your own field of unification. Let the Spirit gradually reestablish the primal harmony in you. Let God's fire consume everything in you that could corrupt its pure gold; let the water from Christ's side wash your robe and your sins. At peace with yourself, you will then be a source of peace for

1 Cor. 3:12–15   others.[16]

75   Build up unity in your community. As a member of the Body of Christ you are called to a work of reconciliation, love and cohesion. Much good would it do you to be a holy solitary, if you were not a leaven of unity! Monks, like saints, are united to God and

[15] Abba Moses.
[16] St Theodore the Studite.

50

to one another through contemplation.[17] Those who live at one with the community and follow the words of scripture, one heart and one soul, deserve the name of monk, that is one alone.[18]

1 Cor. 12:12f.

Where you are, at the heart of the world, detached from all things, be all things to all men so as to gain the greater number through prayer, and so that in the end there may be only one flock and one shepherd.

1 Cor. 9:19
Eph. 2:14f
John 10:16

76   Solitude and unity of this kind cannot, however, be lived without tensions: between father and the brothers; this life and the next; prayer and work; silence and sharing. Don't worry! It is the same in every monastery. It is the same for each true Christian too.

Your vocation must needs pass, as for Jesus, and like his, by way of dismemberment on the cross, due to this twofold love, the price of which must still be paid in blood. Until God allows you to taste in him that perfect unity in perfect diversity at the heart of his mystery of trinitarian love, you will have to stay aware of the twofold demand of solitude and communion. The monk is the man separated from all and united to all.[19]

77   One single word expresses the place where this whole quest for holiness converges: *your heart*.

Where could the monk's treasure be if not deep in his heart? Within you there is a spot closer to you than yourself which you cannot enter without the assent of the One already there. You can only find the way there at the cost of lengthy effort, by the light of great purity, when total destitution is achieved. There God has placed a spark of divinity, the image of his face which has made you in his likeness, the source of living water that can well up in you in everlasting life.

Matt. 6:21
John 4:14

[17] Origen.
[18] St Augustine, *In Ps.* 132:6.
[19] Evagrius Ponticus, *De Oratione* 124.

God made your heart large enough to contain it. But since that heart holds the One whom the whole universe cannot contain, it is therefore greater than the universe. The creator of the world lives in your heart and with him the whole world.

Astonished, fascinated and dazzled by this revelation, the monk sets to work with a will to descend into the depths of his heart. Man's true pilgrimage, he knows, is inwards: there is, somewhere in him, a point where the beginning rejoins the end, where the Eternal meets with Time; where an immortal truth was inscribed in him before the world was created, destined to survive for ever, holy and immaculate in the Father's presence, in love. He knows that the precious pearl is hidden in the middle of this field and off he goes, full of joy, forsaking all, to search this field again.

Matt. 13:44-5

78 You are God's field, God's building. Everything you have and are should be concentrated on discovering this treasure. Truly, the kingdom of heaven is within you. Seek first, seek only the kingdom of God hidden in the depths of your heart, and all the rest will be given you over and above. Because they have grasped this, the monk and nun are people for whom God is enough.

1 Cor. 3:9
Matt. 13:44
Luke 10:11
Matt. 6:33

Through your heart,[20] you will find the short cut to other men. There you will feel nearest the Most High and you will discover the depths of your own nature and at the same time what you have in common with others. Go to the depths of your heart and you will attain the universal. There from now on your life is established with Christ in the Father's heart. There your life is most completely incarnate in the heart of the world for God. And there, in the perfect unity of the same God, you will come to know how truly all men are your brothers.

Eph. 4:13

[20] St Dorotheus of Gaza.

52

79   Either you are a monk to the bottom of your heart or you are no monk at all.

Contemplate the pierced heart of Christ. It will teach you the immense love God bears you. Let yourself, like Mary, be invaded by his Word, a piercing sword keener than any two-edged sword; let the word of God penetrate you as deep as the division of soul and spirit, joints and marrow, to assay the thoughts and purposes of your heart. Then all secrets will lie open before you in a way you could never have dreamed. There in your inmost centre the Spirit will scrutinise all, even the depths of God's nature!

John 19:37
Luke 2:35
Heb. 4:12
1 Cor. 2:9–10

The true monk, like the true believer, is such inwardly, in his heart, not according to the letter but according to the Spirit. Such a man receives his commendation, not from men but from God.

Rom. 2:29

At the heart of the city, live in the depths of your heart and you will be a true monk in the heart of God!

7   Chastity

80

1 John 4:8
Ps. 18:27

Love chastity, for it is the path that leads to your meeting with God. God is Love because he is pure. He is pure because he is One, one in pure Love, one in the purity that radiates perfect Love.

True love comes to you through chastity. That is the way God will lead you from relationship to unity, from fruitfulness to life, from pleasure to infinite happiness.

In the contemplation of *Trinitarian love* you will discover that true love illuminates the mystery of your own chastity. By no other means will you get beyond dry moralism or cold stoicism. When God, the Church and the monastic life call you to chastity it is so that you can love.

81

Heb. 12:29
1 Cor. 3:13
Jas. 3:17
Gen. 2:7
Mark 7:14–23
Rom. 14:14–20
1 Cor. 3:15
Luke 12:49
Isa. 33:14

Since your God is a consuming fire, you cannot approach him without being consumed. Since the wisdom from on high is purity above all you cannot taste it unless you have been purified. Let yourself be remade, then, by the one who has already made you. Only the Holy Spirit, who wants to become fire and light in you, can enlighten you and cleanse you from within where the secret of all purity lies hidden. Although nothing is of itself impure, nothing can become pure again in you except by fire. Chastity is this rugged, joyous passage through God's fire.

Like every Christian you are called to chaste love.

You are in the midst of a world disrupted by sin, its primal beauty polluted even in your inmost nature, where your own heart is divided. Like every other human being you will experience the struggle between the flesh and the Spirit and find you are unable to do what you want to do. This fight has to be accepted though there will be days when you catch yourself saying, What a wretched man I am! Who will rescue me from this body doomed to death?

Matt. 15:18
Gal. 5:17
Rom. 7:24

82   Beyond the apparent absurdity and the pain of your struggle, perhaps in your very groaning, chaste love will open your heart to the light of true freedom.

2 Cor. 5:2

Be courageous enough to declare openly that your chastity is partly *sacrifice*, but be glad that this discipline is leading you to sanctity. Whereas sexual indulgence reduces persons to mere objects, obscuring love and ultimately making it a sad business, chastity will help you give up the transitory and illusory. It will show you the true face of life. On some days, perhaps, you will wonder, How can a young man keep pure? Believe then that God is there, acting and thinking in you to make you pure and irreproachable at the heart of a world where you and your brothers are intended to shine as a source of light.

2 Pet. 2:13f.
Ps. 119:9
Phil. 2:13–15

83   Beyond the struggle and renunciation, chastity will lead you to *peace and fruition*. Through it you will perceive the traces of the Spirit in the flesh, the presence of the universal in the beloved, in every face the reflection of sublime beauty, and in the depths of your being the welling up of the divine source. Busy yourself with what is pure, stand upright as God's servant by virtue of purity. Be brave and sing his praises.

John 1:14
Isa. 58:11
John 4:14
Phil. 4:8
2 Cor. 6:6

84   Monastic life calls you to *consecrated celibacy*.

In the footsteps of Christ who was born of a virgin, blessed among women, and who freely chose not to marry, you are called to follow him, forsaking everything, including husband, wife, children, even your own life.

Luke 1:42;
9:23
Matt. 19:27f.
Luke 14:26

As a disciple you do not differ from your master and when you are a perfect disciple you will be like him. Your virginity lived in him will make you a silent

55

and powerful witness to Jesus Christ. By it you will be led into ever deeper aloneness with the Alone, but in the name of a supreme love, that for your Lord and God, whose risen beauty fascinates you. You are then truly a monk or nun before men and before God. At the risk of saying what may sound rather crazy, you are betrothed to a unique husband, like a chaste virgin to be offered to Christ. For this the Lord has seduced you and you have let yourself be seduced, and he has led you into the desert to speak to your heart.

Luke 6:40
John 20:28
2 Cor. 11:2
Jer. 20:7
Hos. 2:16

85   Outside this vital perspective, your consecrated celibacy would lose its value, significance and joy. But lived in the certitude of this Presence, you will taste the deep and peaceful happiness of knowing you are truly and lawfully betrothed to God forever in tenderness and love.

Hos. 2:21

To this gift of love you will then be able to add the power of *witness*. For Christ calls you to live in this way for the sake of the kingdom of heaven. Your self-giving will proclaim your faith. It will affirm, not being of this world, your hope for a new heaven and a new earth filled with justice according to his promise—the world to come where we shall be resurrected, no longer as wife or husband, but like the angels in heaven, our whole being flooded with eternal happiness.

Matt. 19:12
John 15:19
2 Pet. 3:13
Mark 12:25
Isa. 54:1–10

Consecrated to this expectation and this love, your life should testify humbly, gladly and boldly to the hope you have placed in the living God.

1 Tim. 4:10

86   Your choice of virginity should open your whole heart, soul, body and mind to God's love. God is worth all! Your thoughts, words and deeds should be filled with the love of God in whom all things are gathered up, and your creator will be your spouse.

Maybe one day as your purity and surrender grow, you will provoke the unfailing love of the Lord to become specially desirous of your beauty. The meaning of God's jealous love will dawn on you and you will grasp something of the joy of the divine spouse promised to your soul, and glimpse the inextinguishable delight of the wedding feast to which God himself invites you. Do not try to explain this! Let those understand who can! If God lets you taste him, enjoy him in secret, and your peaceful joy will speak for itself.

Luke 10:27
Col. 3:17
Isa. 54:5
Ps. 45:12
S. of S. 4:7
Deut. 4:24
Eph. 5:27
Rev. 21:2
Matt. 19:12;
6:6

87   Consecrated celibacy should make you open to the world, totally available and all things to all men, free to love everyone and no one in particular. Be careful not to cultivate special friendships that might become exclusive but, free like Christ, make yourself all things to all men and a friend to mankind.

1 Cor. 9:22
Col. 3:11
Isa. 41:8

Virginity will teach you the secret of thoughtfulness and the value of respect, and that universal eternal love is possible.

You have chosen it freely, so offer it for those who have to bear it unwillingly, as if your flesh is making up what is wanting to the Passion of Christ for the sake of his Body the Church. Be humble in your chastity. You are what you are by the grace of God and your consecration is due to his grace alone.

Col. 1:24
1 Cor. 15:10

88   Your consecrated celibacy is not a denial of your body but a fruition, by giving it its deepest and ultimate meaning in the likeness of the Word made flesh, who calls all to become one Body. Since your body is the temple of the Holy Spirit and you do not belong to yourself, glorify God in your own body. Not only is your body for the Lord which is marvellous enough, but the Lord is for your body and this is exhilarating to the highest degree. God lives in you and you in him and, seeing this gift of God, live fully your own gift to him.

John 1:14
1 Cor. 12:12;
6:19–20, 13
John 6:56;
4:10

For love of chastity let your heart expand in the light and joy promised by Jesus to the pure of heart, who will see God. Through him, your life will radiate a Presence, will reveal the secret of an intimacy, will

57

draw on itself for a secret dynamism: the peace of true
fruitfulness.

Matt. 5:8

89   Like *Mary*, virgin, wife and mother, your virginity will bring you to the mystery of a true betrothal, real paternity and loving maternity; as the husband draws joy from his wife so God will take joy in you.

Isa. 62:5

Being poor, virginity will liberate you. Humble, it will make you mature. Childless, you will become fruitful. Sing aloud for joy, O barren woman who never bore a child: the barren woman has seven children and the mother of many sons is left to languish.

Isa. 54:1
1 Sam. 2:5

90   However great and inspiring this ideal, it can only be lived by God's grace and in answer to his call.

Heb. 13:4
Eph. 5:32

Marriage, too, is a way to sanctity and you should in no sense look down on it, for it is a great mystery.

Do not commit yourself to the way of consecrated celibacy unless you feel explicitly *called to it by God*. It is not for you to choose as an ideal but to respond to as a call. But do not let fear of its difficulties frighten you even so.

John 15:16

If you are called by God, he will see to it that it becomes easy and makes you happy.[1] But on condition you live it to the full. Nothing would be worse in this matter than half-measures. If your celibacy is to be a light burden it must be entire.

91   Be neither tense nor slack. Live without vain regrets or compromise. Like a traveller and foreigner, abstain from fleshly desires that war against the soul. Fighting and falling, do not lose heart even so. In the evening tears and at dawn cries of joy. What you have given to God is no trifle, but he knows this. When you are tempted, he will give you grace to bear it. No one is tempted beyond his strength.

1 Pet. 2:11
Ps. 30:6
1 Cor. 10:13
Jas. 1:13–14

Penance and the Eucharist will be your daily

[1] Pope Paul VI.

strength, and Mary, the mother of tenderness, will teach you the secret of fair love.

Your friendships should be neither unwise nor prudish; neither naïve, nor nervous.

92   Among your consecrated brothers and sisters be full of respect and tactfulness in your mutual prayer and brotherly affection. It is such a grace to go forward, brothers and sisters together, sharing the same ideal and the same friendship, that for nothing in the world should you risk its undoing. In this matter be absolutely limpid and you will avoid mistakes.

Purify your memory; keep watch over your thoughts, control your words; wear the habit to show your consecration. Do not try either to be noticed or ignored.   Eph. 5:4

You are not meant to run away but to climb. Do not grieve over what you leave behind, rejoice over what you have received. Avoid evil by doing good. Love better by loving more.   1 Thess. 5:22

Your city is in the heavens from whence you eagerly await the coming of the Lord Jesus Christ. He will transfigure your wretched body and give it a form like that of his own resplendent body, by the very power which enables him to make all things subject to himself.   Phil. 3:21

Believe joyfully in the resurrection of the body professed in the Creed.

Be chaste and you will be happy.

Be pure and you will see God.

8 Poverty

93
To acquire true riches,
to escape the illusion of false treasure,
and to tread freely and joyfully in Christ's
footprints,
you have chosen to be betrothed to *Poverty*.

Because you are both a victim of sin and guilty of sin, you cannot draw near to God without first turning away from yourself and the world. You will be enriched neither by your old nature and its tricks nor by the deceitful appearance of this passing world. Man in his riches does not understand, he is like the cattle whose life cannot last. May your poverty turn you from illusion and the burdens of the glittering world about you and lead you to the true freedom of detachment and the joy of the hundredfold in this present life.

Rom. 5:12
Col. 3:9
1 Cor. 7:31
Ps. 49:13
Gal. 5:1
Mark 10:30

You are called to pass through that narrow gate barred to the rich, so that you may have total and endless possession of a true treasure and eternal heritage. For God has chosen those who are poor in the eyes of the world but rich in faith to be heirs to the kingdom promised to those who love him. May this vision of hope illuminate and cheer you on your way so that you remain ever conscious of the wisdom that guides your steps. And may God give you the perception to see the hope contained in his call and the treasures of grace in his heritage among the saints.

Matt. 7:13;
19:24; 13:44;
19:21
Ps. 37:18
Jas. 2:5
Prov. 28:11
1 Cor. 1:26–7
Eph. 1:18

94
From now on your road to true riches leads by way of the Passover of poverty. Go after Christ, then, who was rich but became poor to enrich you with his poverty. God leads the poor aright and teaches them

60

the way. If you understand that, you will be ready to lose everything to gain Christ. Instead of a theory, an exercise or even an ideal, your poverty has become a *face*: the face of God become poor for you in Jesus Christ. By contemplating this face, you will grasp the true meaning of the mystery of poverty.

2 Cor. 8;9
Ps. 25:9
Phil. 3:8

> Lean on this wisdom.
> Take strength from this hope.
> Contemplate this face, to become like it.

And so you will begin to be poor like him, ready to give and to receive, anything and everything. To give everything for love and receive everything in humility.

Luke 9:23–5

95   The first stage of your Passover of poverty is the *humble acceptance of your wealth*.

No matter what you do or say, you are rich in your faith, hope, love of the Fraternity, your culture, health, freedom and even in knowing why you thirst for poverty. Do not let this make you feel either ashamed or vain; God has no favourites. Do not feel guilty about it, but never forget it.

Acts 10:34
Rom. 2:11
Gal. 2:6
Prov. 13:7

In return continually thank God and, since you have nothing that you have not received, let poverty lead you to offer ceaseless sacrifice of praise. Live humbly, for you may not glory in what comes from God alone and not from you. Nor can you foresee to what hiddenness and deprivation God may want to lead you tomorrow, in the steps of the One who was brought to nothing for our sake. Be ready, then, and thankful, and you will have taken the first step into the mystery of poverty.

Eph. 5:4
1 Cor. 4:7
Heb. 13:15
John 5:44
Phil. 2:7

96   The second step along this road consists in the *giving up of your material belongings*.

You were born naked and you will return as you came. So be willing to be separated from the merely transitory and artificial. Free yourself personally from

61

every possession. The root of all evil is the love of money. Uproot yourself. If you want to be perfect, go and sell all you possess, give it to the poor and you will have treasure in heaven. How could you become rich for God while you go on heaping up possessions for yourself? Material poverty begins by courageous and radical detachment, and this depends on you alone. Live accordingly, with no half-measures.

Eccles. 5:14
1 Tim. 6:10
Matt. 19:21
Luke 12:33

In Fraternity you may *possess nothing of your own.* Do not keep gold or silver or even small change other than what is allowed by the Rule. Each salary is to be handed in, entirely, to the community and the slightest expense incurred openly and under orders. This is the way you will learn freedom and how to fix your eyes on invisible things that alone are eternal. For where your treasure is, there your heart will be.

Matt. 10:9
2 Cor. 4:18
Matt. 6:21

97 As a group, our rule is to *own nothing whatever.* We do not need a heritage in the land because God himself is our inheritance. We should be content, like most people today, to rent a house or to accept hospitality, as promised to disciples of the Gospel. God alone suffices[1] and for us this is a magnificent heritage. In a world of insidious materialism, only radical living of the Gospel can impress. By the foolishness of this message God has willed to save those who believe it.

Num. 18:20
Mark 6:10–11
Ps. 16:5–6
1 Cor. 1:21

Live this detachment, personal and communal, joyfully and without regret. Thus freed, use things in the spirit of detachment, giving thanks to God, like Job, repeating; Naked I came from my mother's womb and naked I shall return. God has given and God has taken back: blessed be the name of the Lord! And you will find rest for your soul.

1 Cor. 7:31
Job 1:21
Matt. 11:29

98 In the community you will *share everything* with your brothers and sisters: money, clothes (given when you entered, and received, as time goes by, from whoever is in charge of clothing), books (to be taken

[1] St Teresa of Avila.

to the communal library at once), and anything else considered of use to the Fraternity. Keep nothing for yourself without the prior's consent. Stifle in yourself all acquisitiveness, for even a single thread will prevent the bird from taking wing.[2] And say over and over in your heart, All that is mine is yours. Like the first Christian communities in Jerusalem where everything was held in common and shared according to needs, build up the holy temple with your brothers.

Heb. 13:16
Luke 15:31
Acts 2:44–5

99 Material poverty in community is also shown by simplicity of housing, meals, clothing, transport, furniture and so on. Be content with your salary. Eat what is set before you and learn to be completely self-sufficient, equally content to have plenty or to be in want. Taking nothing for your journey, follow the Son of God who had nowhere to lay his head. Leave the dead to bury their dead and, without looking back (which would make you unfit for the kingdom), become a monk travelling along the *pilgrim's way* like a stranger here below. Let your *steadfastness*, grafted and pruned by God, and your faithful, wholehearted commitment to your new family be your only riches.

In a word: Go. Sell. Give. Come. Follow Christ. These words should be so many landmarks along the road of detachment from the world and attachment to Christ, this twofold demand being the whole essence of the monastic life.

Luke 3:14;
10:8
Phil. 4:11–12
Luke 9:3;
10:4; 9:57–62
1 Pet. 2:11
John 15:2–4

Luke 18:22

100 The third stage opens you to the *poverty of solidarity*.
Having in a certain sense bound yourself to dependence on and to the constraints of the big city you will have to sacrifice the joy of silence, the beauty of nature, the peace of the countryside, the natural rhythm of days, green things and pure air . . . Regret nothing! Simply live a twofold solidarity: with Jesus, who chose first to belong to the town of Nazareth and then to the city of Jerusalem, where at times he seemed not to belong to himself at all; with all men

Luke 2:51;
13:33
Mark 10:32

[2] St John of the Cross.

Mark 3:20;
2:1–2; 6:31
who, today, are more and more subject to the endless constraints of city-life of which you are aware.

Beside the poverty that renounces the world by forsaking it, live the poverty that is bound up with the world, yet be free from it. Be a son of the Church in the everyday world, the battlefield where God is present.

John 17:15–18
Isa. 60:14

101

The fourth stage of your Passover leads you to *poverty of affections*.

When Christ asked you to forsake home and property, father, mother, wife, brother, sister, relatives and friends, he invited you to sacrifice your heart to him.

Luke 14:26
Matt. 19:29
Luke 12:34

For no love, attachment or relationship may come before the one you must bear to God if you are to be worthy of him. For he was the first to hate his life for our sake: the Father giving you his Son and the Son losing his life for us all.

Rom. 5:6
Matt. 10:37
Rom. 8:32
John 15:13

Only grace can give you insight into the mystery of this jealous God who demands everything because he is more than everything, and who can already satisfy you completely here below.

Exod. 34:14
Luke 18:30

Surrender your affections, whether they be good or unruly. Purify even your memory, your recollections and secret desires and you will see your stony heart become a heart of flesh and your heart of flesh a new heart, bearer of a new Spirit. Share with your brothers a heart wide enough to contain one single love, soul and spirit.

Ezek. 36:26;
11:19
Phil. 2:2

If, therefore, your hand is your undoing, cut it off; or your eye, tear it out. But always bearing in mind that God wants love, not sacrifice, let your self-denial be humble and unobtrusive. The Lord detests a poor proud man. The reward for passing through this crucible will be love enriched with all the intensity of a poor, joyous, purified heart; of a faithful heart. Go and seek out some poor, loyal-hearted man.

Mark 9:45–7
Matt. 9:13
Ecclus. 25:2
Tobit 2:2

102   You will then be able to cross the threshold of *spiritual poverty*.

This is the highest degree of poverty. It should lead you to surrender your self-will, thoughts, intelligence and self-love, as you follow Christ whose nourishment was to do his Father's will. Give yourself up entirely to this. Lay down your arms. Lose yourself in total immolation. This is the kind of spiritual poverty Christ proposes. Henceforth, if the Spirit is leading you, let the Spirit dictate your actions too.

John 12:49–50
Matt. 5:3
Gal. 5:16, 25

Material poverty is easy enough. Shared poverty is hard. Poverty of affections is always painful. Spiritual poverty crucifies.

Gal. 6:14
1 Cor. 2:2

It is the highest degree of your Passover of poverty, since it will lead you to the lowest place. After stripping yourself of all your possessions, then of other people, you now have to strip yourself of yourself. Not merely to renounce but to repudiate yourself. But Christ is with you on the road.

Luke 9:23
Matt. 16:21–7

The reward of such giving is entry into the Father's will. You are no longer a slave to any man, but a son. And being nothing, everything will come to you. Stripped bare, the kingdom is your wealth. You are God's heir and co-heir with Christ. The Spirit in person joins himself to your spirit to attest that you are a child of God. The Father and you are one, since you do what pleases him.

Gal. 4–7
Rom. 8:16
John 10:30;
8:29

103   You will not be able to follow Christ in this final stage of his Passover of poverty; the final place is so completely his that no one can ever snatch it from him.[3] But you should be tireless in contemplating this emptying, burial and annihilation of the man who became slave and sin for you. True God born of true God, he is the slain lamb, object of scorn, the scum of humanity, a worm and no man. Go ahead, with eyes fixed on the leader of your faith and guide to perfection, Jesus, who instead of the joy set before him endured the cross to its very extremity for your sake.

Phil. 2:6–11
2 Cor. 5:21
Rev. 5:6
Isa. 53:3
Ps. 22:7
Heb. 12:2
1 Pet. 3:19

[3] Charles de Foucauld.

Enlightening, stimulating and supportive, this contemplation will prepare you for the supreme gift of your own annihilation, burial and total stripping in the Passover of your ultimate death. On that day you will be able to give all. And it will depend on the way you have prepared yourself now. God grant you may not wait till death to die!

So death works its way in you to sow the seed of life around you. Within yourself you bear your death-sentence so that you may learn to rely, not on yourself, but on God who raises from the dead. The Lord is ever at the right hand of the poor; he gives to the poor and his justice is for ever.

May this be your road to poverty and it will be a true Passover for you.

1 Cor. 15:37
John 12:24

2 Cor. 4:12;
1:9
Ps. 109:31
2 Cor. 9:9

9 Obedience

104   The perfect model of obedience is in the mystery of the Trinity. Between Father, Son and Spirit there is nothing but listening, receiving and giving, and from this total dependence flows utter freedom. For respect for diversity leads to perfect communion. So if you want to understand the basic reason for your obedience, contemplate the Trinity.

Obedience is no human invention but the expression of God's very being. What he wants you to grasp is not a relationship of dependence, submission or even conciliation, but a free relationship of love.

Christ, the Son of God and perfect man who so loved us, became obedient precisely for this. What the old Adam and you yourself have refused, the new Adam took on himself for you. Son as he was, he learnt from what he suffered to obey. If then you wish to be perfect, remember Jesus Christ; your master was the first to obey, and you can be no different. As disciple, you should be content to become like your master, and a servant like your Lord.

John 15:9
Phil. 2:8
Rom. 5:19
Heb. 5:8
2 Tim. 2:8
Matt. 10:24

105   Through obedience you will learn to love: to renounce self, so as to do what is pleasing to your brothers and to God; to love your neighbour as yourself and God before all; to unite with others for common action, by listening to one another in accordance with God's plan. The Father thus expects you to co-operate freely in his design of love and your brothers expect you to participate freely in the communion of this love. The more you obey, the more you love; and the more you love, the more you will live obediently; for love and obedience are one and the same thing. So if you want to love, be obedient.

Luke 10:27
1 Pet. 1:22

Your obedience will testify to your faith. You, a sinner, obey sinful men and in so doing choose to look beyond appearances. At times things will seem incomprehensible or hard, but it is through these trials that your love will be expressed, when you have to forge forward in the darkness of faith. Such a test of faith is the only proof of your love.

John 12:35–6

106 Through obedience you will live your poverty: that radical poverty of abandoning your own will, thought and self-love. More than non-possession, this perfect obedience will make you a truly poor man, nourished like Christ by God's will alone.

John 4:34

Obedience will teach you freedom and truth. If indeed you obey the commandments, you will then know the truth and this truth will make you free. By accepting the fact that God's thoughts are not your thoughts and his ways are not your ways, you will have eyes to see, even though you may not understand. The Spirit from within will lead you into all truth.

John 8:32
Isa. 55:8
Deut. 29:3
Mark 8:18
John 16:13

Obedience will teach you about mercy, for, overriding your rebelliousness, sloth and stubbornness, obedience will take you back to God, whose tenderness and forgiveness will bring you peace. Even should your heart condemn you, God is greater than your heart. This is the way you learn that all is grace and that with God nothing is impossible.

1 John 3:20
Luke 1:37
Matt. 19:26

107 Joy and peace will come to you by obedience. It will not diminish you but, quite the contrary, when you obey you are not belittled, but enlarged. The love of God dwells in you and his will guiding your life will pacify and fill it with happiness. You know in whom you have believed. Then you will have reached such detachment that your journeying will go on endlessly. For your route is not predetermined, but God himself is leading you along the road to eternal life. Obedience seeks to enlighten your whole being. Be utterly open to it and the light will shine even in your face. The Lord's commands are limpid, giving light to the eyes.

Ps.139:24; 19:9

Finally, obedience will make a true son. The Father will, henceforth, be able to speak to your open, available and liberated heart as to his own Son. And the new Spirit that obedience has brought into your heart of flesh will enable you to make bold to use the most affectionate of names you could possibly utter: Abba! Father! Son in the Son, you will see the Father, and he will listen to you and love you.

Ezek. 36:26
Rom. 8:15
John 14:9,
13–23

108 True obedience, then, is above all a conversion. Turn away by obedience from your old nature and the world and turn towards the realities on high and the search for God deep within. Thus, purified and stripped, you will become transparent to his will.

Col. 3:1

True obedience is both listening and acting, and this supposes attentive docility on your part. Listen, come to God, and your soul will be able to live and put all this into practice.

Isa. 55:3
Luke 8:21;
11:28
Jas. 1:23

Obedience is prompt and undivided. True monks immediately put aside their own concerns, abandon their own will and lay down whatever they have in hand, leaving it unfinished . . . This obedience, however, will only be acceptable to God and to men if the order is carried out fearlessly, promptly, eagerly, without grumbling or word of objection.[1] Meditate on these words of the great master of obedience. Put them into practice and you will become perfect in the image of the Son.

Matt. 5:48

109 In obedience there is no arguing nor superficiality. Nor is it sporadic or half-hearted. Obedience should take hold of you completely. Give yourself up to it thoroughly and for ever.

Obedience in words only is not real obedience. Genuine obedience must reflect sincere dependence on and true surrender to the decision awaited and received. What would it be worth if you only obeyed

[1] St Benedict, *Rule* 5.

when this fitted in with your wishes and will? When obedience starts to be hard, then it becomes the most true.

110

You are to obey God and God alone.

For he is your only master, guide, Father and Lord. Knowing his limitless love for you and that he is the all-powerful God, you can choose nothing finer than to follow the loving plan he has drawn up for you, by doing his will in all things. So say, Amen to God's glory. Whether it suits you or not, obey the voice of the Lord your God and obedience to his Word will make you happy.

Obey the Father for he loves you. It is good to obey this Holy God and spend your remaining time according to his divine will.

Obey the Son for he is the source of salvation for those who obey him, and you have been sanctified by the Spirit to hear Jesus Christ. If you love him you will observe his commands by subjecting all your thoughts to obedience to Christ.

Obey the Spirit by becoming docile to his voice, for it is to those who obey that God gives his Holy Spirit to lead them gently, through him, to the fullness of truth and true fruition.

By obeying God you will enter into the joy of the Trinity and enjoy peace.

Matt. 23:8–10
John 13:13
Exod. 34:14
1 Cor. 8:6
Eph. 4:6
Matt. 6:10
2 Cor. 1:20
Jer. 42:6

John 16:27
Ecclus. 46:10
1 Pet. 4:2

Heb. 5:9
1 Pet. 1:2
John 15:10–14;
14:15
2 Cor. 10:5

Acts 5:32
John 16:13
Gal. 5:22

111

You have also to obey your brothers who, with you, make up the Body of Christ and the Temple of the Spirit. When you truly obey you become holy and able to love one another sincerely as brothers. The communion of listening to one another will reveal the will of God, who is in your midst. With your brothers, strive for one love, one soul and one mind and you will build up a solid temple by means of the Holy Spirit speaking through the praying community.

The Fraternity is Christ. Let God speak through it at Chapter. Be submissive and truly obedient to decisions, be they small or great, which then become the community guidelines.

Matt. 18:20
Phil. 2:2

112 Be more especially obedient to the person the brothers freely choose and recognize as servant of authority to express the voice of the community and the very will of God. Make yourself loved by the community, and be self-effacing before its leader. Your wholehearted readiness to obey will increase the grace of God in him. With your prior and prioress be truly obedient and really open in all ways.   Ecclus. 4:7

Then there will be an exchange of love and faith between the one who serves by commanding and you who serve by obeying. Even in trifles, do everything in the light of this obedience. In this call to holiness you will find the freedom of a purified heart and the mature joy of a surrendered spirit.   1Thess. 5:12–13

The man who commands you is a sinner and you, still imperfect, obey. Yet through this twofold expression of the imperfection of master and disciple you will be led into the way of perfection,[2] where you will never lack grace as long as you are trustful, open and persevering.

Be faithful till death and Christ will give you the crown of life.   Rev. 2:10

113 THE PRIOR (PRIORESS)

Authority is God's instrument to lead you to good.   Rom. 13:4

1. The very name *prior* tells you he is *first*. Not in the hierarchical order of precedence or even of sanctity but the 'first one to obey'. The first to want to submit to the rule that the Fraternity has accepted and, by that very fact, the one to stimulate the whole community. The first to want to do the will of the Father and to remind you of it.   Matt. 20:28

2. Therefore, he is a chosen one; elected as the one whom his brothers have chosen to take on this responsibility, and either chosen or ratified by the Church as well. This twofold mediation enables you to recognize the prior as also blessed by God, and the Lord's chosen one. Guided by the Spirit, the choice and prayer of the brothers bestow on this man, in spite of his shortcomings, a special grace of state;

---

[2] St John of the Cross.

71

henceforth, when you listen to him you will hear more than this voice. Acknowledge in him what he represents rather than what he is.

114

3. He should, however, be a model. Not *the* model (only Jesus is that). But one whose very life bears witness. What he must be is genuine; and you are asked to see him for what he has become. Nothing will be more inspiring to the brothers than to be spurred on to sanctity, and nothing will better convert the prior than the obedience of a true disciple. Single-minded authority will lead you to real obedience, and single-minded obedience on your part will make for just authority. When the prior sees in what spirit his brothers choose to obey, he cannot fail to be converted.

Phil. 3:17
1 Pet. 1:15

4. The prior is essentially a servant. Authority is service, and he exercises his charge in the name of and in the eyes of all. Servant of the servants of God in the likeness of Christ who, being first, came not to be served but to serve. The fundamental duty of the prior is thus in his turn to be the first servant.

Mark 10:45
Luke 22:27
John 13:14

5. Above all he has to be a good listener. Listening to God from above in prayer and hearing this same God speak here below to the whole community and to each brother individually. He must listen so as to be better informed, better to speak, answer, discern, guide and correct. His is the attentive ear at the place where the Word coming from God and the echoes arising from his and the Fraternity's consciences converge. Listen to him and make yourself heard.

115

6. This brother has a kind of personal charism of the Son of God. An especially son-like quality is recognized in him, enabling him to draw each of his brothers to the same filial behaviour towards the one who alone bears the name of Father. His charism is to develop the various gifts of the whole body, giving them cohesion and harmony in the grace of the Holy

Spirit. Through him, place your charism at the service of the community. Matt. 23:9
1 Cor. 12:1–11

7. He is a peacemaker. The one who is to co-ordinate and reconcile different personalities, tendencies, inner aspirations and outward calls, bringing them all to a consensus. This unity needs to be embodied in a single person, the better to mould the brothers into a single body. The prior should not stifle individual personalities but gather them together. He remains the bond of unity between the various members of the community even if he is—and he will be—dismembered himself in the process.

116   8. The prior is also the guarantor of the Rule chosen by the brothers and of the main orientations of the Fraternity's vocation. He guides the Fraternity towards its agreed goal. He sees that what has been written down does not become a dead letter. Hence, when necessary, he explains, reminds, corrects and supports. But always keeping in mind that the spiritual life is movement and that he is to guide a pilgrimage rather than defend a fort or administer an estate. The monk is pilgrim as much as watchman. 2 Tim. 4:2

9. Simply by being himself, the prior exercises a function. His task is to be prior and he should be able to take up this charge effectively. It is no mere mystical or spiritual role but one in which he has to administer a body, share responsibilities and respect those of others. 1 Pet. 5:1–4

10. To him especially falls the task of discernment, helped by the brothers in office. In this matter he has a leading role, since many of the decisions and directions which have to be taken depend partly on him. To assist him he has a council, a master of novices and a cellarer to share offices and responsibilities.

117   11. Since the prior's job is to assume authority, his authority must, in fact, be exercised. This will not be done without pain nor without perhaps causing suffering to others. But the worst enemy of the common good is either abdication (on the part of authority) or demagogy (on the part of the community) which could open the door to every kind of division, individualism and fantasy. On the other hand, authority that is courageous, firm, gentle and humble, strong yet tender, will liberate, stimulate and clarify. The prior has to occupy his place; excactly that, but nothing more. And he must command.

Rom. 13:1–4

12. He makes demands but sows joy and peace. The adventure, led like this, should be an adventure to holiness. But only on condition the atmosphere is trustful, joyous and serene. As a man of peace, the prior should spread peace, and as a bearer of joy he should communicate joy. His vocation as *first* is, in fact, a call to holiness. Over and above all, he must love.

Rom. 15:13

Let him pray unceasingly for all his brothers and every day you, brother, should pray that he may receive the double charism of a listening and discerning heart as you search together for the will of God.

Matt. 6:10

10 Humility

118   Humility is the soul of monastic life.

Humility is not one of the courses of a feast but the condiment that seasons all the plates.[1] Silence, obedience, fasts and vigils, work and self-discipline all lead to humility by which the rejection of all self-sufficiency and thirst for power may be rooted in our hearts; and Christ, who is only Love, may be born again in each of us.

Pride leads to disobedience, through which sin entered into the world and, through sin, death. The first degree of humility is obedience[2] and obedience restores us to life.

Rom. 5:12
Gen. 3:5
Heb. 5:9

The Lord himself teaches you how to acquire perfect humility when he says, Learn of me for I am meek and humble of heart, and you will find rest for your soul. If then, you want to acquire perfect humility, see what Jesus endured and endure the same.[3] Humility is Jesus Christ who came down from heaven not to do his own will but the will of the one who sent him. This is the lesson your Saviour and Master gives you so that you may do as he did, who came not to be served but to serve. If you tread in his footsteps you will penetrate the great mystery of the humility of God, who made himself the servant and redeemer of us sinners, the witness to limitless Love.

Matt. 11:29
John 6:38;
13:14–15
Matt. 20:28
Isa. 53
Rom. 5:8

119   Humility should remind you first that you are only a *creature*. Remember that your strength is from the Lord. Like Peter, acknowledge that you too are

[1] *Sentences of the Desert Fathers*.
[2] St Benedict, *Rule* 5.
[3] Barsanuphius, *Correspondence* 150.

only a man, mortal man like everyone else. And that
to be pleasing to God, the greater you are, the more
humble you should be, for so great is his power, he
is honoured by the humble. Be willing, then, to be a
mere creature before God, and through such fear you
will penetrate his secrets.

Deut. 8:17
Acts 10:26
Wisd. 7:1
Ecclus.
3:18–20
Ps. 25:14

Humility should also remind you that you are still
a sinner.

That it is the grace of God that makes you what
you are. You know there is nothing good in you, that
is, in your flesh; for though you may wish to act well
you cannot do what you want. Mindful of the basic
incapacity that leads you ceaselessly to murmur, Lord
Jesus, Son of the living God, have mercy on me a
sinner!, banish from your life every vestige of pride.
He did not come to call the righteous but sinners.
Humble repentance alone can justify you. You carry
your treasure in an earthenware pot, so that everyone
may see that this extraordinary power comes from
God not you. Go on repeating with the tax-collector
and centurion of the gospel, Lord, I am not worthy
to have you under my roof, Jesus, have pity on me a
sinner. It is better to be a man who sees his sins than
someone who raises the dead to life by prayer. The
man who knows his own weakness is greater than the
one who contemplates the angels.[4]

1 Cor. 15:10
Rom. 7:18
Matt. 9:13
2 Pet. 3:9
2 Cor. 4:7
Luke 7:6;
18:13

120 So humility will become the grace of *conversion* for
you.

To train and sanctify his people the Lord tested
them with humiliation. Recall the way the Lord led
you for forty years in the wilds to humiliate you and
test you and discover what was in your heart. Before
you were humbled you went astray; now attend to his
promise. The Father wants to lead you along the same
way, to help you progress, for he corrects the man he
loves and chastises every son who pleases him. The
Scriptures say, There is not a man on earth who is so
righteous that he never sins.

Deut. 8:2
Ps. 119:67
Heb. 12:6
Eccles. 7:20

The way of humility, then, passes through *humili-*

4 Isaac the Syrian.

76

ation and there will be days when it will seem a fiery furnace. Be convinced that disdain and slights are medicine against your pride, and pray for those excellent doctors who ill-treat you. Of one thing you may be sure, the man who hates humiliations hates humility.[5] In temptation, lower yourself still more and God will help you. You will be advancing along the way to true perfection and your ascent will be proportionate to your abasement. For every man who lowers himself will be raised up and the man who raises himself will be lowered. Isn't it the sign of true humility to rejoice in insults? Like all Christ's disciples called to lose themselves for his sake, happy are you if in the end you can say, We are merely servants, we have done no more than our duty. Along this road you will be actively advancing towards that good passivity that will make you ready and flexible to grace; so that, humbled under God's powerful hand, he may raise you up when the time comes.

1 Pet. 4:12
Wisd. 3:6
Jas. 1:13–14
Luke 18:14
Matt. 5:11
Acts 5:41
Luke 17:20
1 Pet. 5:6

121   By this very fact humility will teach you *holiness*.
    The devils know only too well that humility is the gateway to perfection, so that, according to the desert Fathers, they dread it more than any other virtue. One day the devil said to Macarius, I can't fight you. And yet, everything you do, I do. You fast and I never eat at all; you watch and I never sleep. But you get the better of me in one thing. What is that?, asked Macarius. Your humility, replied the devil. Surely this is the way Jesus himself overcame his adversary. Nothing so much as humility casts out and overcomes devils. Humility is their ruin.[6]

Matt. 11:29

122   For this reason humility requires constant *watchfulness*.
    Watchfulness over thoughts, wants and desires. Be aware at every instant that you are under the eye of God in heaven, before whom your every action is laid

[5] St Dorotheus of Gaza.
[6] *Apophthegmata.*

77

bare.[7] And through this fear, you will humbly learn to receive from God a share in his vigilant holiness. It is a great grace to live constantly aware of God's gaze on you. Humbly consent to be sounded to the depths, to be scrutinized in your most trivial thoughts, and he himself will guide and protect you. Seek the Lord, you humble of the land, seek humility and perhaps on the day of his wrath you will be sheltered beyond all fear.

Ps. 139:2, 16
Zeph. 2:3
1 John 4

And so humility will carry you on to *perfect love*.

First, to that perfect love of God, by which all fear is forever banished, so great is the joy of knowing that you, once humiliated and contrite, though still a sinner, have been washed, forgiven and reinstated, no longer as a servant but as a friend of the God who raises the humble. Remember, all labour is ruin without humility, for humility is the forerunner of charity. John was the forerunner of Jesus and drew everyone to Him. In the same way humility attracts love, that is, God himself, for God is love.[8]

John 15:15
Luke 1:52

Love of others will follow. If each brother, through humility, thinks others better than himself, there will be no place among the brothers for faction or for vain glory: jealousy, discord and rivalry will be banished.

Phil. 2:3
1 Pet. 3:8–9

123 Humility, gentleness and patience make bearing with others a happy thing, since mutual contacts are enveloped in meekness. The joy of communion is born of this mutual submission, which is especially due to obedience. Understood in this way it becomes, as in Christ, openness to love. Whoever wants to be first among you let him be at everyone's beck and call and the one who aspires to high position be your servant. Then he will grasp the meaning of humble love combining tenderness, respect, affability and gentleness, imprinted with a joyful and serene gravity.

Eph. 4:2
1 Pet. 5:5
Luke 22:27
Mark 10:43–4

Humility finally leads you to the right kind of *love of self*. It reconciles us with what we are. Don't think too well of yourself but judge yourself fairly. Though

[7] St Benedict, *Rule* 7.
[8] *Apophthegmata*.

God humiliates, he does not despise us, and when he humbles us, he does so to raise us up. True humility should teach you that if you are nothing on your own, through God you are everything: heir of Christ, co-heir of divine glory and sharer in the divine nature.

Rom. 12:3
Luke 18:9–14
Rom. 8:17
2 Pet. 1:4

124 True humility never despairs of God's love. Like Christ who was gentle and humble of heart, whom God exalted, the wise and humble man can walk with uplifted head. Deeply aware of his nothingness, from the depths of his abasement and lowliness, and now beyond discouragement, the dismantling of self and the trials by which God has broken him, he remembers that having yielded to mercy, the Father's love has raised him up. Self-perfection is not of interest to him now. Put to death by God, in him he lives.

Ecclus. 11:1
Phil. 2:8–9
Jas. 4:10

Let annhilation lead you to this exaltation. Descend to the very bottom of this slope. Unless you die you cannot see God. And for your sake God made himself lower than you. If you die to yourself by humility, you will find him there in the depths of your being and you will live eternally. The Lord exalts the humble, of whom the first is Mary. He leads them righteously. Be humble and you too will possess the land, enjoying a great peace.

Exod. 33:20
Job 5:11
Luke 1:48
Ps. 36:11

125 Two ancient Fathers in particular will travel with you along this road to humility with their wisdom and teaching: St John Cassian and St Benedict.

ACCORDING TO CASSIAN

Here are the signs by which you can recognize humility:

First, if the monk is dead to self-will.

Second, if he hides nothing from his superior, not only his actions but also his thoughts.

Third, if he trusts his own judgement in nothing, but puts himself totally into the hands of his superior, eager for his advice that he listens to with joy.

Fourth, if he obeys in all things with gentleness, ever maintaining constant patience.

Fifth, if he not only does no harm to anyone but is not upset or saddened by insults he himself receives.

Sixth, if he dares to do nothing but what is authorized by the common rule of the monastery or the example of the ancients.

Seventh, if he is satisfied with all that lowers him, and in all tasks given him considers himself a poor and unworthy workman.

Eighth, if he proclaims, not only with his lips, but believes in the depths of his heart, himself to be the least of all.

Ninth, if he controls his tongue and avoids loud talk.

Tenth, if he is neither inclined nor quick to loud laughter.

These marks and other similar ones are the signs of *true humility* and, when you truly possess it, it will lead you ever higher till you reach the perfect love that casts out all fear.[9]

126 ACCORDING TO BENEDICT

Now the ladder of humility is our life on earth which the Lord will raise to heaven, if we humble our hearts.[10]

Twelve steps mark this ascent, which is an ever deeper abasement.

1. That a man lives in the fear and sight of God from whom nothing is ever hidden. He must be humbly submissive and constantly vigilant.

2. That a man loves not his own will nor takes pleasure in the satisfaction of his desires.

3. That a man submits to his superior in all obedience.

4. That in this obedience, under difficult, unfavourable or even unjust conditions, his heart quietly embraces suffering and endures without weakening or seeking escape.

[9] John Cassian, *Institutions*.
[10] St Benedict, *Rule* 7.

5. That a man does not conceal from his abbot any sinful thoughts entering his heart or any wrongs committed in secret.

6. That a monk is content with the lowest and most menial treatment.

7. That a man not only admits with his tongue but is also convinced in his heart that he is inferior to all and of less value.

8. That a man does only what is endorsed by the common rule of the monastery.

9. That a man controls his tongue and remains silent, to keep from sin.

10. That he is not given to ready laughter.

11. That a monk speak gently, seriously, briefly, wisely and quietly.

12. *Then* his whole being will be invaded and as it were impregnated by humility.

Having climbed all these steps of humility, the monk will quickly arrive at that perfect love of God which casts out fear . . . All this the Lord will, by the Holy Spirit, graciously manifest in his workman now cleansed of vices and sins.

127   At the end of our Passover, we are promised a share in divine glory. But the last stage on this road for all of us leads to the final step of abasement. On that day, to rise to heaven, we shall have to descend into the earth. To be drawn to heaven by the Father, you will be lowered into the earth by your brothers. Your whole journey should be lit up and understood in the light of this vision of the twofold state of abandonment to which you will then be reduced. Monk and nun, from the very start see yourself on this last step and let what you see be the luminous guide for your whole life. For at that moment you will in very truth be *alone with the One*. John 17:24; 6:44

The earth from which you were made will take you. God alone can raise you up and grant you life in *his* presence. All pride is thus in ruin. Contemplate your existence from the standpoint of your last day on earth. Humility is the gate to glory and this is the monk's wisdom and his life.

81

If you die with Christ, with him you will live.

2 Tim.
2:11–12 If you hold firm to humility, with him you will reign.

OF JERUSALEM

11 In the Heart of the City

128 Get up, go into the city and you will be told what to do.

Since one of the main features of our time is the urbanization of our great modern cities, an essential characteristic of your monastic vocation today is to be a *city-dweller*.

Acts 9:6

From earliest times the city has concealed a twofold secret of good and evil, holiness and sin.

Positively, it represents one of the privileged meeting-places between God and man. Dwelt in, sanctified, consoled and made joyful by the Lord, it is faithful, radiant, holy, rebuilt, restored and repopulated by the grace of the Most High. The city received his only Son who taught in its streets, instituted the Eucharist, rose again, sent his Spirit forth to found the Church, all within its precincts. And there in the city he is waiting to return in glory, a new Emmanuel, to live forever among men and share with them the happiness of eternal love.[1]

The city is the place of shared prayer and love, and the ultimate ground that will receive the new garden within its heart forever. You should love and mediate on the mystery of the city. For God himself chose, built, saved and sanctified it. The best of man's intelligence, labour and faith has been put into it. Hence, you can live in God's heart at the heart of the city because it is his dwelling-place. Be monk and nun in the very heart of the city of God.

Rev. 22:2
Isa. 60:14

[1] Biblical references for this paragraph in sequence: Wisd. 9:8; Neh. 11:1; Baruch 4:30–6; Zech. 8:3; Lam. 2:15; Isa. 52:1; Jer. 30:18; Ezek. 36:35, 10; Luke 13:33; John 7:15; Mark 14:13; Acts 1:3; Acts 2; Rev. 21:23; Isa. 35:10; Rev. 21:2–3.

129 Conversely, the city is the place of human pride, noise, idolatry, sin, massacre and distress. It provokes the death of the prophets, the condemnation of the Son of God, the scandal of the cross planted near its ramparts under the eyes of the populace and, finally, ruin and shame.[2]

You will have to wage a twofold fight in the heart of the city: for God and against evil. There you will receive a double grace: a meeting with God and purification from your own sins. In the city you will have to struggle and contemplate. What the early monks set out to seek yesterday in the desert, you will find today in the city.

All monastic life is a fight and urban monasticism calls for fighters. Jesus came to bring not peace but the sword.

Matt. 10:34

Oppose eroticism, prestige and money, with the firm contrast of a life of poverty, humility and purity. Fight noise with your silence; weariness with your peace; endless comings and goings with your repose in God. No cloister will protect your prayer; the countryside will not bring you serenity; the walls of your enclosure will not preserve your virtue. Followers of Christ, the Beatitudes summon you to a life of real struggle in the heart of the city.

1 Tim.
6:11–15

130 Learn, too, to contemplate the beauty and holiness of the city where God resides and where he has placed you. There, at the heart of the city, raise your arms in praise and intercession. Call down his blessing on it each day and praise the Most High for all holy men and women who live in it and sanctify it.

Faced with so much loneliness, with such tragic cases of isolation, live with your brothers that true solitude that God's grace fills with joy; that true communion that prayer extends beyond all separations and absences. Day by day the city will test, purify and sanctify you. And you, like God, will espouse it.

[2] Gen. 11:4; Jer. 13:9; Isa. 22:13–14; Ezek. 8; Baruch 4:8; 2 Kings 14:13; Jer. 14; Luke 13:34; Mark 10:33; Luke 23:27–35; 21:24.

It is as much in need of you as you of it. The Lord
himself returns to the city and means to live in the
midst of Jerusalem!

Rev. 21:3
Zech. 8:3

There have always been, and still are, monks and
nuns (Carthusians, for instance) who live in the heart
of the city. They are praying there with you. They
are praying there for you. Like them, pray in, with
and for your city.

Stay in the city until you are clothed with strength
from on high.

Luke 24:49

131   Furthermore, *today* a new world is emerging:
yesterday mainly rural, today almost wholly urban.
Your life therefore corresponds to a particularly real
and urgent appeal from the world, the Church and
God himself.

Believe that monastic life is not incompatible with
the urban phenomenon of our day. The desert is now
inside the city too. Like all those witnesses who
became Jews with the Jews, Greeks with the Greeks
and outlaws with the outlawed, be a city-dweller with
the city-dwellers of today.

1 Cor. 9:20–1

The adaptation of forms by fixed means within an
unchanging purpose has always been characteristic of
monks. They have never been afraid of putting old
values to new uses. This same freedom should be
yours when occasion dictates: *Nova et vetera*.

At the heart of the city the monastic calling makes
you and your brothers and sisters the living and
humble witnesses—among many others—to the
hidden God. Hence, your welcoming of every man or
woman of good will who cares to join you, morning,
noon and night, in contemplating God. There God
invites every man to seek him, for all are heirs,
members of the same body and receivers of the same
promise in Christ Jesus through the Gospel.

Eph. 3:6

132   In the midst of the desert through the labour of
prayer, conversion and penance, the monk and nun
create *an oasis*. If grace causes the living water to

surge up, you should know how to share it in the name of the sacred law of the desert and the holy law of monastic hospitality which says: if you meet a thirsty man give him water. Do not create enemies for yourself by refusing to share water from the rock. The genuine monk is not afraid of being disturbed.[3] No need to be indifferent, in order to be holy. Do not be unkind because you want to be separate. Even if your enemy is thirsty, give him something to drink. Let the thirsty man come, the man of desire, and receive the water of life as a free gift. At the last judgement you will not be asked if you drank well but if you shared well. Nor if you often said: Lord, Lord!, but if you practised charity. Nor if you fled from men, but if you served them. Freely you have received, so give freely.

Isa. 21:14
Rom. 12:20
Rev. 22:17
Matt. 25; 10:8

The primary axis of your whole life should be the search for God and at all costs you should safeguard silence, prayer, spiritual reading, community life, solitude and rest. But your rhythm of life must correspond to the *rhythm of the city*, Be first and foremost a monk, but an urban monk. Solely a monk, but at the heart of the city. Work in the city, pray in the city, work and pray for the city, weep and sing with the city.

133   Like most city-dwellers who take the weekend off, do not be afraid to spend one day a week in the desert. Just as they have their holidays, take your retreat times. This is vital for your brothers and sisters as well as for you. Adopt a similar pattern, but live it with a difference. Do not go to bed too late or get up too early. The city is tiring but you have to endure. Find your own rhythm.

Avoid unsettling visits outside, and distracting television at home. Give up theatres and cinemas once and for all. This is part of the necessary break. But be well-informed, open to others, attentive to the city's cries for help. You have to live communion this way too.

[3] Apophthegmata.

But do not identify yourself with the city to the point of melting into it. It is not so much a question of rooting yourself more firmly in it as of teaching its inhabitants how best to prepare their own uprooting from it. For they too are longing for a better country—I mean a heavenly one—which is why God is not ashamed to be called their God, for he has founded another city for them! Let your life proclaim to those who dwell in the heart of the city that they are all on the pathway to the heart of our God.

Heb. 11:13–16

134   If the Lord gives you grace and you stay faithful to it, the city will not destroy your monastic vocation. On the contrary it will strengthen and develop it.

You want solitude? The city is one vast solitude.

Isa. 24:10

You want to live in communion? In the city everything is gathered into one.

Ps. 122:3

You want to be holy? The city is holy.

Isa. 52:1

Holy once it is washed in the blood of Christ crucified.

Matt. 27:53

Holy because one day he will make it his beloved bride.

Rev. 21:2

To be a witness, go into the city: she is called Faithful.

Isa. 1:26

To be righteous, go to her: she is called Righteousness.

Isa. 1:26

If the monk is a sacred minister, the temple where God resides is in the midst of the city.

Ps. 11:4

If he is a martyr, Jerusalem kills the prophets and stones those sent by God.

Luke 13:34

You want to anticipate heaven? Heaven is a city.

Rev. 21:2

To enjoy your God? He has created the city of joy for you.

Isa. 65:18

Do you want to see God? The angel shows you the holy city come down from God above.

Rev. 21:10

You want to meet him face to face? God lives in the city.

Ps. 135:2

To be absorbed in God? Be a monk in the city of God.

Isa. 60:14

135

Mark 14:24
Luke 22:44
John 19:34

The blood of the Lamb was shed over the city.
The blood of the chalice, the blood of his forehead and side.

Acts 2:3–5
John 12:28

On the city descended the fire of the Holy Spirit.
Through the city echoes the Word of the Father.
In the city Jesus fought the devil and overcame him
Matt. 4:5 for good.

In the city Mary lived, Jesus taught, the apostles evangelized preaching repentance, beginning with
Luke 24:47 Jerusalem.

The prophets prophesied in the city, the priests offered sacrifice, the wise men spoke there.
Luke 24:48 The witnesses bore testimony in the city.

The lover of the Song sought her Beloved in the
S. of S. 3:3 streets of the city.

Could the city lack *Watchmen*?

For Zion's sake I will not be silent . . . I have posted watchmen on your walls, Jerusalem, who are
Isa. 62:1–6 never to be silent, day nor night!

12 At the Heart of the World

136   The holy monk is the one who is with the world in his desert, and in the desert when he is in the world.[1]

The search for God, the uniquely necessary, takes place through man, for he is the image of God, the Body of Christ and the Temple of the Spirit. In this impermanent world God alone suffices: but God came into the world and he has put us in it too. Christ carried on an unceasing struggle with the world's outrages and yet with an ever-deepening incarnation in the heart of everyday reality. Hence, as a monk, you are also called to follow and serve him and seek God's face exactly there where he is to be found: which is at the heart of the world, where you must continue fighting the same battle that he fought. When you become monk or nun, Jesus does not ask you first to withdraw from the world, but to keep yourself from evil. As the Father sent Jesus into the world, so you also are sent into the world. This is the will and Testament of the Son of God made man.

Wisd. 2:23
1 Cor. 12;
3:16–17
Wisd. 13:1–5
John 15:18–20
Acts 17:27–8
John 16:33;
17:15, 18

137   However, you cannot seek God and mature fully unless you keep yourself from this passing world and make use of it as though not using it. If we belong to God, we cannot at the same time belong to the world. As the saying goes: Friendship for the world is enmity to God; and if anyone loves the world, the love of the Father is not in him. For the whole world lies in the power of the evil one. You cannot serve two worlds at once. Hence, Christ's warning that this necessary break with the world may lead to strife, misunderstanding and even rejection. If you belonged to the

[1] A hermit of Mount Athos.

91

1 Cor. 7:31
1 John 4:5–6
Jas. 4:4
1 John 2:15
John 5:41–4
1 John 5:19
Matt. 6:24
John 15:19–20
1 John 4:1–6

world, the world would love you well. But as you do not belong to the world, since my choice has drawn you from the world, the world hates you. Remember what I said: the servant is not greater than his master. The essence of your monastic life is, and remains, flight from the world; flight from the spirit of the world, but immersion in its reality.

138   Your whole monastic responsibility is to keep yourself from the world without cutting yourself off: to be part of it but not absorbed in it. By this twofold commandment of love you will be judged. One of the most difficult tasks for monks is to reach a harmonious *balance* between *presence* in the world and *detachment* from the world: both being necessary if they are to act as a sign of the kingdom, which is what the Church and the world itself expect of them.[2] Your life has to be hidden, but not obscure. Live it openly in face of God and man like Jesus in Nazareth, without your break with the world becoming contempt, your retreat forgetfulness or your solitude misanthropy. Quite the contrary, do all you have to do without complaint or wrangling. Show yourselves guileless and above reproach, faultless children of God in a warped and crooked generation, in which you shine like stars in a darkened world and proffer the Word of Life. Your awareness of God's presence does not depend on your remoteness from the sons of God but on your openheartedness towards God. Love, not hate, distinguishes you from the world. Hence, never be acidly ascetic, disdainfully self-sufficient or savagely solitary: all things that go to make up the so-called bad monk.[3]

Matt. 5:14–15
Luke 2:51–2
Phil. 2:15–16

139   Generations of forebears will teach you this: monks have always known how to be close at hand yet keeping their distance, bound up with other men yet solitary,[4] attentive to men's needs[5] while yearning

[2] Pope Paul VI.
[3] Olivier Clément, *Questions sur l'Homme.*
[4] St Basil, *Longer Rule* 3, 7, 20.
[5] St Benedict, *Rule* 53, 58, 61.

for God alone. Adapting to eras, events and civilizations, they have made their contribution to the work of the world. Following their example and walking in their footsteps, you have to discover your own happy mean between an indispensable break and a necessary communion; how to flee truly and totally from the spirit of the world, though remaining bodily within it. To be at one and the same time Martha and Mary.[6]

Do not regard withdrawal from the world as the be-all and end-all, by supposing that your meeting with God and your holiness will be assured by mere virtue of isolation or solitude. Holy monks[7] and even hermits[8] warn you severely against this. The desert or habitual retreat far from the world are not in themselves graces but only means. You can carry the whole world with you into a solitary life, and can live truly alone with God Alone in the heart of the everyday world. So never fight to retain old structures, but fight the true fight of faith in the depths of your heart. Faith gives endurance; do not be proud but fearful rather, and persist in the state in which you were when God's call came to you.

1 John 2:15–16
John 3:16–17;
12:46

John 8:29;
16:32
1 Tim. 1:18;
6:12
Rom. 11:20
1 Cor. 7:17;
20:24

140 Even so, you know that no one can embrace the monastic life unless he forsakes all he holds most dear, to seek out places of silence, to live intervals of solitude and attend only to the things of God. So be convinced that perhaps you serve this world better by distancing yourself from it a little, for thus, by your life, you will remind it of its long-term direction and ultimate need, and you will offer it the support of your prayers. It is good for the world that you admit you are useless. The world needs monks who forsake it, to make it think, to question its assumptions.

More fundamentally, in the heart of God who created, redeemed and loved the world so much you will recover the whole universe. You could not poss-

Luke 14:25–7;
17:10
John 16:7

---

[6] Aelred of Rielvaux, *Sermon on the Assumption.*
[7] St Basil, *Longer Rule* 6, 7.
[8] Philoxenus of Mabbag.

ibly be nearer the world than by living constantly in its Creator's presence.

In the immense fellowship of the Church and the great monastic family, live your own charism as complementary to that of others: rejoicing that others, in their own different ways, are living their own forms of membership and solitude; then humbly accepting your own limitations as regards nearness and distance from the world. Experience, life and the Spirit will gradually show you the true nature of your own charism and the individual richness of the spirituality of Jerusalem. Perhaps this will primarily prove to be a spirituality of dismemberment. But isn't that the Cross?

141   To live the perfect balance, which only Jesus achieved, always be careful to avoid the twofold snare of indifference and integration. Too far cut off and distanced from the world, your life would no longer be monastic; but exaggerated conformity or closeness would make it even less so. On the one hand, you must reject the world, as the Scripture says: Do not love the world or anything in the world. On the other, you must love the world, as the same apostle writes: He who does not love his brother whom he sees, will be unable to love the God whom he does not see. The God who loved the world so much that he gave it his only Son! So if you stand apart from the world, it must not be to condemn it, but so that it may be saved by Christ whom you meet in it. Only a very great love can entertain a just contempt for the world. You forsake it and separate yourself from it only the better to find it and serve it in God. There is no end to learning how to love!

1 John 2:15, 4:20
John 3:16, 17

Lastly, never forget that the community you live in is that privileged portion of the universe where you are to settle. Your monastery should be the first of all places where your love, hospitality, joy, work, fervour, praise and peace are lived and shared. To be in the world means just that: to reveal and find God at its heart, in renewed awareness of its primal beauty and in joyful anticipation of its happiness to come. In the desert of the urban world your monastery should thus be an oasis of peace, prayer and joy; an epiphany of God's love.

142   Two things have traditionally helped monks and nuns to find their right place and make themselves felt, as regards their presence in and distance from the world: enclosure and the habit.

No walled *enclosure* surrounds the boundaries of your monastic existence. Do not regret what you would find hard to justify by anything written in the Gospel. It is for you to set up a moral enclosure round your life. Keep a strict watch over those times and places when you should be alone with God, or meeting with the community.

Watch over your eyes: the lamp of your body is your eye. If your eye is healthy, your whole body will be in the light; but if it is sick, your whole body will be in darkness.   Matt. 6:22–3

Watch over your lips: may the Lord set a muzzle on your mouth and keep watch at the door of your lips.   Ps. 141:3

Watch over your hands: if your hand is an occasion for sin cut it off.   Mark 9:43

Watch over your steps: if your foot is an occasion for sin cut it off.   Mark 9:45

Watch over those you meet: do not sit down with rogues or mix with hypocrites.   Ps. 26:4
                                                                    Ecclus. 9

Watch over your heart: where your treasure is there is your heart.   Matt. 6:21

Wear nothing but the armour of faith and love, with the helmet of the hope of salvation. Then you will not be afraid at having the city as your enclosure.   1 Thess. 5:8
For this city will be inhabited eternally.   Jer. 17:25

Jerusalem is to remain without walls, said God, I shall be a wall of fire around her and I shall glory in her midst.   Zech. 2:4–5

143 To live and make this presence and distance felt, your belonging to God and your separation from the world within the world, wear a *monastic habit*.

Always and everywhere, even outside the bounds of Christendom, monks and nuns have worn a habit, enveloping their prayer, manifesting their poverty, signifying their consecration and their perpetual and total belonging to the Lord, expressing their simple life and community of mind. For you it is the same. Love this symbol of communion with the Fathers and of the legacy of their spirit, which you, in your own way combining new and old, are carrying on today.

But do not try to be more monastic than the monks and, when you go out to work, like them, if necessary and if the community agrees, wear working clothes. At all other times wear the habit that you have been given.

With the East, believe that the habit makes the monk. With the West, remember that the habit alone is not enough. Clothe your body and dress your heart. Live in your habit. Monks and nuns, our habit reminds us all that we are consecrated men and women.

144 In your cowl, you celebrate the divine liturgy. In the monastic habit, celebrate the liturgy of the habit, of the cell, of the chapter, of the monastery. Your whole life is liturgy.

Let it symbolize your belonging to Christ and that you are his, completely and forever! Yes, you have been bought—at what a price! Yes, we have been sold to him. But this was for love. Nun, you are Christ's spouse. Monk, you are Christ's disciple. All you, in fact, who have been baptized in Christ *have put on Christ*. You, the Lord declares, are my witnesses and servants, whom I have chosen. If you learn to wear your monastic habit unashamed and without murmuring it will be your road to freedom and joy, the gateway into the self-emptying of Christ and pathway to his glory.

Do not be afraid of looking dreary: joy is in the eye.

1 Cor. 7:23,22
2 Cor. 11:2
John 15:8
Gal. 3:27
Isa. 43:10

Ps. 19:9
Prov. 15:30

Do not regret being anonymous: God calls you to be a witness.

Do not fear being a challenge: believers and unbelievers alike expect you to be brave in silently, joyfully manifesting your faith.

If you are despised remember that Christ was despised before you.

Do not be afraid of all being dressed alike or of looking different; the world at large submits to the far more capricious tyranny of fashion. Learn freedom from all that!

Isa. 43:10

John 15:18–19
Luke 10:16

145   This habit was none of your choosing; you received it; hence it opens the way to poverty, humility and obedience. Do not value it for more than it is worth but see it as a *test* foreshadowing far more vital renunciations that monastic life will offer you. One day, God will ask you like Abraham not only to forsake everything to walk before him, but to sacrifice him your Isaac. You have not as yet been blooded in your struggle against sin!

Separated from all and united to all, monk or nun at the heart of the world, clothed in his beauty, sing the glory of the Lord!

Gen. 22:2
Heb. 12:4

Baruch 5:1–2
Isa. 61:10

13   In the Church

146   Outside the Church no one can be a monk.

Every authentic monastic life implies a true belonging to the Church.

For one thing, the monastic vocation cannot develop except within the framework of Church life; for another, its meaning can only be fully grasped within the mystery of the Church. You should then both meditate on this mystery, and delve into this reality. And in contemplating this most beautiful of all divine works, Holy Church, you will find what you need to enlighten and support you along your daily, laborious road to God.

·The mystery of the Church is that of a new people redeemed by the blood of the Lamb, making all the baptized become sons in his Son, fellow-citizens with the saints, and members of God's household. Quickened by the Spirit, this holy people is united in Christ to come through him *to the Father*.

Eph. 2:19
1 Pet. 2:9
Eph. 2:18

147   *In Christ* who redeemed, founded and sanctified her, the whole structure of the Church adjusts herself to grow into a holy temple. In him, each individual is made part of the building to become God's dwelling in the Spirit. To bring this great mystery about, the very mystery of the body of Christ—for we are the body of Christ, each of us being a different part—the Church continues the presence, worship and mission of Christ in the world by associating herself with this sacrifice of him who offered himself to the Father for the life of the world.

Eph. 2:21–2
1 Cor.
12:12–30
Heb. 2:10–18

Monk and nun, since your purpose is to seek the face of Christ in order to give him your life and be the more closely united to his sacrifice, you are a privileged member of the Church.

Col. 1:24
Eph. 1:11–12

The builder of this living unity is the Spirit, who is also the life and strength of God's people, the bond of its fellowship, the energy of its mission, the source of its multiple gifts, of its admirable harmony, of the light and beauty of its creative power, and the flame of its love.[1] We have all been baptized in the one Spirit to form but one Body; for we have all drunk of the same Spirit.

1 Cor. 12:13

Monk and nun, if you are to live under the influence of the Spirit, who should guide your whole life, you must live at the heart of God's Church.

148 So it is through the Church, with her and in her, that you share in life in Christ and life in the Spirit. And as there is but one Body and one Spirit, so for you there is only one Hope in terms of the call you have received: that of the Church your mother. This communion of saints in the unity of the Church and the faith is such that, believing in the same God, reborn in one baptism, fortified by one Holy Spirit, we are all raised by the grace of adoption to the one life eternal.[2]

Eph. 4:4

We then commune in the Holy Spirit if we love the Church, and we love her if we hold to her unity in charity.[3] The more you are of the Church, the more your life will be centred in Christ and vitalized by the Spirit, and the more monastic it will be. Holy Church is the Body of Christ, a single Spirit quickens it, unifies it in faith and sanctifies it . . . So, monk, when you become a Christian, you become a member of Christ, a member of the Body of Christ, a sharer in the Church and in the Spirit of Christ.[4]

Thus you have access to the grace of God through Holy Church, which simultaneously signifies his Pres-

---

[1] *Lumen Gentium* (Vatican II) 4, 7, 9, 12, 18, 21.
[2] St Peter Damian.
[3] St Augustine.
[4] Hugh of St Victor, *De Sacramentis* II:1,2.

ence and transmits his Life to you, becoming a *sacra-mental reality* for you.

149   As you meditate on the mystery of the Church, the mystery of life and unity, of the meeting of God in man and of man in God, you will find the inner sap that has vitalized monastic life ever since its origins. Mother Church will teach you how to listen to the Word, practise interior prayer, love unity passion-ately, be loyal to the faith, be constant in your own mission, serve your brothers and repent in humility. Such are some of the typical virtues making up the monastic life.[5] Through the Church, you will love your monastic sanctification and vocation, at the heart of the *Fraternity of Jerusalem*.

Your monastic life, then, is to follow Christ, within the Church. By professing the evangelical counsels of poverty, chastity and obedience, by promising to change your ways and pray continually, by commit-ting yourself to set aside any likely obstacle to charity and the perfection of divine worship,[6] you undertake to carry to its ultimate consequences the common baptismal calling to life in the Spirit.

The monk dedicates himself to God by an act of supreme love and is committed to the honour and service of God under a new and special title . . . joining him to the Church and her mystery in a special way.[7] So much so, that there is a definite bond between the monastic life and the life of the Church, between monastic sanctity and the Church's sanctity.[8] Your monastic state therefore is not situated between that of the cleric and that of the layman, but derives from both the one and the other constituting a special gift for the whole Church.[9] By it you participate in a particular way, by consecration, in the sacramental nature of the people of God.[10]

[5] *Relations between Bishops and Religious* 4.
[6] ibid. 10.
[7] *Lumen Gentium* 44.
[8] ibid.
[9] ibid. 43.
[10] *Relations between Bishops and Religious* 10.

150   Let your monastic vocation then make you a visible witness to the fact that you belong to God. By this vocation within the Church, offer the world a visible sign of the ineffable mystery of Christ and the incomparable riches of his love for you, surpassing all understanding. By it bear public witness in the Church-as-Sacrament that the world cannot be transfigured and offered to God except in the spirit of the Beatitudes.[11] By it, lastly, with your consecrated brothers and sisters enrich the Church with this special charism, that has its place in the harmony of the whole Body. Be attentive and faithful to your twofold mission of silent witness and life in the Spirit, a mission at once charismatic and apostolic. The Lord wants you to be a discreet but authentic witness of the most absolute value of all.   Eph. 3:19

By your life of asceticism and denial, share in the suffering Church.

By the witness of a life proclaiming that God alone is enough, share in the Church militant.

By all that your life anticipates now of the kingdom of heaven, and by the bond that your worship establishes with the saints in heaven, share in the Church triumphant.

Let your whole monastic vocation be thus centred on the great mystery of the Church.

151   *The link with the episcopate* should characterize your belonging to the Church.

The Church is the people united with its pastor; the bishop is in the Church and the Church in the bishop.[12] Such centuries-old traditional teaching may not be gainsaid today.

The Lord himself instituted various ministries in his Church for the good of the whole body.[13] Among these, the episcopate is fundamental to all the others. In the Church no one but the bishop exercises so

[11] *Lumen Gentium* 31.
[12] St Cyprian.
[13] *Lumen Gentium* 18.

fundamental a function of fecundity,[14] unity,[15] spiritual power,[16] and sanctification over all ecclesiastical activity.[17]

152   Our monastic vocation lies midway between the privilege of exemption and the confines of priesthood, in *a fundamental bond with the local Church* in the person of its pastor.

It is not for us to create a church within the Church but to be a church cell in the one holy Church. In this respect, live the letter and spirit laid down in the statutes of your Fraternity; they safeguard the necessary independence of your specifically monastic vocation while at the same time showing that you belong to the local church by which you exist, which you serve and to which you pertain.

Have faith in the rich theological developments in this field, and so find the deep sap of your roots. Your attention to, and availability to, the hierarchy will promote grace in them, which will fall back on you. By converting your contemplative vocation you will convert the hierarchy to contemplation. In this, have no historical or sociological regrets. A filial spirit of dependence in faith will be your best means of enduring and enriching your monastic identity in which, rest assured, the bishops believe as much as you do! And if this should seem doubtful, your obedience will be worth all the rest and your deference will lead them finally to give you their full confidence and trust.

153   The Church herself founded the monastic family of Jerusalem, setting it on an already existing foundation, that is, Jesus Christ. The brother known as *the founder* is no more than a useless instrument. But God willed he should be necessary. The founder's charism is an experience of the Spirit transmitted to

[14] ibid. 19.
[15] ibid. 23.
[16] ibid. 22.
[17] *Relations between Bishops and Religious* 6.

his disciples, to be lived, guarded, deepened and developed by them continually, in harmony with the Body of Christ, in unending growth. Hence, the Church defends and upholds the charism proper to each foundation.[18]

1 Cor. 3:11
Acts 9:15
Rom. 15:17

Recognize your brother founder as the servant of the Church of Christ and also as someone through whom your Fraternity has received a special grace; recognize his particular charism by which God has spoken to you in the Spirit, and accept it. By setting this elder brother in his rightful place you will be giving him his full due and, despite his human weakness, you will strengthen yourself in the holiness of the Church of Christ, whose servant he is.[19]

Luke 17:10

Aim then to listen to two voices: that of Christ through the episcopate and that of the Spirit through the charism of the foundation.[20] In such a way both the spiritual and hierarchical aspects of the organic communion of the Church draw their origin and strength from Christ and his Spirit.[21]

Eph. 2:20–2

154   The bishop at the head of your Fraternity represents Christ.

He is the one to discern whether a foundation is opportune, and permits, establishes, protects and guides it.[22]

He approves and ratifies the rule of life it is to follow.[23]

He institutes the monastic family to which you belong, by conferring on it the dignity of a canonical state of life.[24]

He watches over its growth, to see that it develops in the spirit of its original charism.[25]

He approves its particular character and specific

[18] *Christus Dominus* (Vatican II) 33, 35.
[19] *Relations between Bishops and Religious* 12.
[20] ibid. 9.
[21] ibid. 5.
[22] *Lumen Gentium* 45.
[23] ibid.
[24] ibid.
[25] ibid.

mission and, according to circumstances, entrusts it with particular tasks and mandates.[26]

In a deeper sense, he consecrates monks and nuns to a higher service of the people of God[27] and presents religious profession as a state of consecration to God.[28]

The bishop, as primary celebrant of the Eucharist, delegates his power to each priest in the monastery, around whom the Eucharistic assembly gathers, and makes the monk a liturgist in the Church of God and in the midst of mankind. Again, because the bishop is one vowed to God and his flock by the gift of his entire life, as such he invited each individual to live this same abandonment to the Father and the brothers.

Government and teaching are subordinate to his call as *perfector*, that is, one who leads others to sanctity.[29]

Finally, he is the representative of the Spouse of Christ whose ring he wears, the chief dispenser of the mysteries of God and artisan of the holiness of his flock in accordance with each individual's recognized vocation.[30]

155   To live your monastic vocation correctly, you must fully grasp the meaning of the episcopal charism. So, listen attentively to your bishop as one who has been placed on your path by Christ himself, to sanctify, teach and govern your life in the ways of the Gospel. If you listen to him, you listen to Christ; despise him and you despise Christ. He for his part will respect your personal vocation and the charism of your community, without taking the place of your founder or of the prior duly elected by the brothers or of the prioress duly elected by the sisters; nor will he interfere in the internal government, discipline, spirituality or worship of the monastic family, which are all matters outside his jurisdiction.[31]

Matt. 18:18;
16:18; 10:40
John 13:20

[26] *Relations between Bishops and Religious* 8.
[27] *Lumen Gentium* 44.
[28] *Sacrosanctum Concilium* (Vatican II) 80:2.
[29] *Lumen Gentium* 25–7.
[30] *Christus Dominus* 15.
[31] *Relations between Bishops and Religious* 130.

156   In this spirit each Fraternity will establish a particular *canonical statute*—or renew the original one—with its local church in the person of the local bishop. If the bishop so desires, he may submit this statute to the Sacred Congregation of Religious in Rome for approval at the appropriate moment.

General statutes will then detail, if necessary, the relationships between all the Fraternities. Should it seem useful, the bishops' conference can appoint a bishop chosen for his doctrinal competence and his understanding of the monastic life, to maintain the fabric of unity and authentic contemplation among the various communities, consistent with the charism characteristic of the monastic family of Jerusalem.

Without becoming dazed by these canonical questions, be aware of their value and importance, and once the statutes have been established, respect them.

157   After this, what will evangelization entail for you in the context of the Church?

First, that you have to proclaim the Gospel by your whole life.[32] The monk evangelizes by striving to live the evangelical counsels radically. By doing this, you will—really and truly—bring a little more peace, mercy, purity, gentleness and justice into the world. This is already a form of evangelization.

Then, by virtue of being concerned primarily with spiritual realities (and secondarily with political, social, economic and cultural matters), you touch what is most real in human life: the inalienable, universal and immortal point that Jesus was the first to call our soul. Of all that is real it is the most real. What does it profit a man if he gain the whole universe if he loses his soul? Let your life tell the world what the evangelist cries, You fool! This very night your soul will be demanded of you; and this hoard of yours, who will get it then? And thus you will show people how to seek the authentic treasure.   Luke 12:20

[32] Charles de Foucauld.

158   The testimony of your shared love, telling in whose name you love, and of your liturgical worship, telling to whom you speak, is your best way of evangelizing a world thirsting to know who is the source of this search and this love. Surely far better than sermons: God is love and only shared love can tell of God. So live in such a way with your brothers and sisters that people can once more say, See how they pray! See how they love one another! and thus be drawn back to the One who is source of this love and prayer.

John 13:35
Acts 2:47;
5:12–14
Matt. 5:16

Finally, believe in the supreme efficacy of intercessory prayer in the work of evangelization and that true contemplatives, in this sense, are not the least of missionaries.

159   So, your function may not be that of a pastor in charge of such and such area or parish but you are none the less a monk apostle wanting to live the apostolic *forsake all*, and choosing to put all in common like the first apostolic communities. This abandoning of all for Christ's sake and this sharing of all in Christ's name are what make the apostle. So, in this sense, too, your monastic vocation is eminently apostolic.

This witnessing to the absolute demands of God, calling you to live your life absolutely in the spirit of the Gospel of Christ, you must live to this end, to the ultimate act of witness. Be a martyr in spirit, die to sin, mortify yourself and you will be pure in spirit and a martyr of Christ.[33] You cannot glory in proclaiming the Gospel, since this is your absolute duty. Yes, woe betide you if you do not preach! Throughout your self-sacrificial life, keep saying, Here I am!

1 Cor. 9:16
Heb. 10:7

By the fervour of its prayer, the reality of its love and the sincerity of its hospitality, let your community be such a cell of the Church as Christ would have it be: one, holy, apostolic and universal, an epiphany of the Lord of Light!

---

[33] *Apophthegmata.*

160   By the dual bond maintained with the local church and with the monastery of S. Benoît-sur-Loire, which has been given you as sponsor, visibly demonstrate that you belong both to the Church of today and to the age-old Tradition, as a true disciple and true son. A son of the Church and a disciple of monasticism. The Church is not your servant but your mother; the monastic ideal is not something to be conquered but to be led into.

Love the Church with intense, mystical and filial love.

Man receives a great and supernatural dignity when he becomes a member of the Church. Marvellous his union with Christ and, through Christ, with God and with all the members of the Church! Sublime mystery of belonging to the Church! As great as that of the mystical Body of Christ, as that of the Eucharist its fulfilment, as that of the Incarnation its foundation, as that of Grace its fruit . . . By entering the Church your consecrated soul becomes the true bride of God's son. . .[34]

---

[34] Matthias–Joseph († 1888), *Mystery of the Church.*

14 Jerusalem

161   Jerusalem is your new name.

A name expresses belonging, reflects a mission, reminds of a requirement.

The name of Jerusalem which you bear henceforth says that you belong totally and forever to the Lord, that your mission is to let yourself be invaded by God's love and to proclaim it by the holiness of your life. *Separated from all, live united to all. At the heart of the city live in the heart of God!*

Because Jerusalem is the city given by God to men and built by men for God, thus becoming the patroness of all the cities of the world, and because your vocation is to be a citizen of it, you are a monk or nun of Jerusalem.

Because Jerusalem is the unique meeting place of men and God and because your life is a quest for this encounter and this growth in him, you are a monk or nun of Jerusalem.

162   Because Jerusalem is the city where Jesus Christ went to worship, teach, die and rise again and because your life consists in following him who was more and more alone before the Alone, you are a monk or nun
John 16:32   of Jerusalem.

Because Jerusalem is the holy place where the Spirit descended on the Church and because the monastic life is a spiritual vocation within the Church, centred on the Gospel of the apostles and the person of Mary, as at that first Pentecost, you are a monk or nun of
Acts 1:13–14   Jerusalem.

Because Jerusalem is the home of the first pre-monastic Christian communities, and because their sharing of love and fervent prayer are the well-springs

108

of your prayerful, brotherly vocation, you are a monk or nun of Jerusalem.

Acts 2:42–7; 4:32–5

163   Because Jerusalem is the place where the three monotheistic religions are wonderfully united yet dramatically divided, and because it is your vocation to live the ecumenical hope of the sons of Abraham in a living bond of communion, you are a monk or nun of Jerusalem.

Finally, because the heavenly Jerusalem is free, our mother and the promise of our ultimate reward, and because our whole monastic life seeks to anticipate our entry into the kingdom, exerting all its strength to do so, you are a monk or nun of Jerusalem.

Gal. 4:26
Rev. 22

The festival best expressing all this, and therefore being the feast of your fraternities, is this holy day of Easter.

Clearly, this name like the name of Christian or son of God, is quite beyond your deserts. So be humble in your awareness of being unworthy to bear it, and do all you can to justify it by living a true life. Be permeated by it, moulded by the grace it confers, and gradually become by virtue of the name which you have received what it reminds you that you are: a son or daughter of your Mother, the New Jerusalem.

Ps. 87:5

164   As you read the Scriptures, as you sing the psalms, as you meditate on the prophets, as you tread in Christ's footsteps in the Gospel, let yourself be *taught by Jerusalem*. This name will become, as it were, a key to the Scriptures for you, an endless call to conversion, repentance, praise, holiness and jubilation!

When you are sad your name will comfort you: Take courage, Jerusalem! He who gave you that name will console you!

Baruch 4:30

When you are tired, it will rouse you: I have posted watchmen on your walls, Jerusalem; they will never be silent day or night.

Isa. 62:6

When you are half-hearted, it will convert you:

Jer. 13:27 Woe betide you, Jerusalem, unclean still! How much longer will you go on like this?

Isa. 66:12 When you are worried it will soothe you: I shall send peace flowing towards Jerusalem like a river.

When you are happy, it will make you even happier: be glad and rejoice for I shall create Jerusalem Joy Isa. 65:18 and her people Gladness.

Throughout life Christ will call you by this name Mark 10:33 to follow him: look, we are going up to Jerusalem!

At the end of life, it will welcome you: I will inscribe on you the name of the city of my God, the New Jerusalem which is coming down from heaven Rev. 3:12 from my God, and my own new name as well.

You received this name in the secret of your heart at the end of a penitential Lent, on Easter night. You received it officially from the Church at the end of the Lent of joy, in the light of Pentecost. May Jerusalem each year spur you on to pursue the twofold journey of self-discipline and praise in memory of the blessed days when this name was given you. In the joy of the risen Christ and the light of the sanctifying Spirit.

165 It would be good if from the original single trunk of Jerusalem, which was founded to fulfil the need for prayer, love, work, silence and sharing in a spirit of chastity, poverty, obedience, humility and joy in an urban context, there were to spread *branches* reinforcing unity by their diversity. Differing types of charism, diversity of vocation, variety of approach depending on the age of the individual: all these things require constant consideration as to the various types of vocation that might fit harmoniously into the one monastic family: not, by any means, to reproduce the entire Church in miniature, but to share freely and open-handedly with those whom the Spirit sends us, so that they too can live at the heart of the city, in the heart of God.

166 *Jerusalem as Upper Room,* inspired both by Carmel and St Benedict, should have the feel of a Benedictine-type community, solidly structured but not too institutionalized, in which liturgy, common life, adoration, time in your cell, paid work, discreet hospitality, each find a harmonious place. . .

Jerusalem as Temple, inspired both by St Basil and St Dominic, should have the attraction of a Basilian community, putting strong emphasis on the brotherly life, activity in the Church, apostolic endeavour with a clearly defined pastoral element to it, while strictly safeguarding the monastic requirements of silence, prayer and solitude.

167   *Jerusalem as Hermitage*, inspired both by St Bruno and Brother Charles, should be open to vocations of brothers or sisters called primarily to silence and solitude, though lived at the heart of the masses in the wilderness of large cities. In monasticism, the eremitical life has always flourished alongside the cenobitic. For this life to be free and fruitful, it should enjoy a real independence, being linked only to the family of Jerusalem as a whole and depending directly on the bishop, the founder and the spiritual father. This very clear-cut, classic and logical distinction will give freedom for individual charisms, and the recognition of complementary vocations will give rise to profound harmony, joy and peace, and true spiritual liberty for everyone.

Associated with each cenobitic community of monks or nuns, there will be brothers or sisters (whose fundamental charism to a more extensive professional, charitable or pastoral commitment has been tasted and recognized) who are accepted as having their own way of life and service to others, as well as pre-postulants (those still searching or students), all being members of the family. As regards their reception and mode of belonging, this should depend on the prior or prioress and the council of the individual Fraternity, in close association with the founder.

168   Lastly, the *Jerusalem Community* should enable layfolk, men and women, celibate or married, of all ages, conditions and backgrounds, to live some of the

essential demands of Jerusalem and its Gospel spirit, while maintaining their family, professional, economic, social, cultural, civic or political commitments.

God willing, such will be the *tree of Jerusalem* in the setting of each local church.

Be glad that your monastic family possesses these varied elements and pray that nothing, in one way or another, whether by excessive boldness or timidity, excessive prudence or impatience, may intervene to hinder the grace of the Lord.

169   That these diversities may harmonize in a dynamic, living communion and not at the mercy of individual caprice, it is important that:

On the one hand, discernment of vocations and approval of membership should be the responsibility of the prior after consultation with the council, or the council of priors, which has an essential role to play. Here, obedience alone can ensure that God's will is done and that unity is safeguarded.

On the other hand, strong bonds of communion should be established between all these communities, or modes of consecrated life, and firmly maintained, that is to say:

† *Book of Life* to maintain the same spirit;

† *Name* to signify the same monastic charism;

† *Liturgy* to express the same contemplative spirituality;

† *Liturgical habit* to indicate the same conservation and the same belonging;

† *Central coordination* to ensure concord and harmony between the communities.

170   And you, brother and sister, do all in your power to love, will, defend and enrich this living unity. And then you will have nothing to fear. Since the Spirit is Gal. 5:25   the source of our life, the Spirit must direct our ways.

From this common trunk the different branches can grow and bear fruit. The diversity of the Fraternities can only strengthen the unity of Jerusalem,

112

because well-established links between each house serve to show that the Spirit which animates them is truly that of the *same monastic family*. But always deeply respectful of the *autonomy of each local church*. Jerusalem is neither an order nor a congregation but a family of Fraternities.

Shout for joy, Jerusalem! Widen the space of your tent, spread your curtains freely, lengthen your ropes, make your pegs firm! For you will burst out to right and left. Your race will repeople cities deserted.

171   What will help you reinforce this unity and stress this belonging is the virtue of *stability*.

First, stability is a Christian virtue. An unstable Christian cannot make a stable monk! By your baptism you belong once and for all to Christ. God is forever faithful. His love has been given you for ever; he has inscribed your name on the palm of his hand. Let his name stay written on your forehead and set on your heart. By this indelible character you are marked by God, grafted into Christ, founded on him, crucified with him and dwelt in by him. Being thus caught, you cannot escape him. Having put your hand to the plough, you cannot turn back. Let your life thus be fastened to Jesus Christ. If you hold firm, with him you will live; for even when you are unfaithful, he remains faithful.[1]

Your monastic stability is thus, in this first instance, your baptismal stability. Always keep Jesus Christ in mind. You have been marked with an indelible seal by the Spirit of the Promise.   Eph. 1:13

172   Stability is also a state of soul. It belongs to the monk and nun to be constant, *persevering*, enduring in trials, tenacious in ordeals. After you have suffered a little, the God of all grace will himself restore,

[1] Biblical references for this paragraph in sequence; Rom. 6:10; Ps. 117:2; 1 Cor. 1:9; 1 John 1:3; Jer. 3:12; Isa. 54:10; 49:16; Deut. 6:6–8; 2 Cor. 1:22; Rom. 11:17; 1 Cor. 3:11; Gal. 6:14; 2:20; Phil. 3:13; Luke 9:62; 2 Tim. 2:11; 13.

confirm, strengthen you and make you unshakeable. In this firmness of hope and faith lies true stability. Aim to be even-tempered, in life's vicissitudes be patient; be calm and live at peace. Let everything about you, your very manner of being, of speaking or walking indicate the poised, emotionally balanced man or woman. In life's ups and downs be at heart serene. Be stable, without wild enthusiasm or undue depression. Stable in your soul; stable in your faith; stable in your choices; stable in your love of God.

Living like this, you will also learn what monastic stability means. In Jerusalem this can hardly be geographical stability since the Fraternities will never own property. But it will reside in your faithful presence in the monastery, your effort to remain in your cell, and your refusal to be always out and about. Happy are those who are not for ever dreaming of other ways or other places, but try to send down firm roots where they are. Only thus will they bear fruit!

Matt. 10:22
Rev. 2:19
2 Pet. 1:5–7
1 Pet. 5:10
Ecclus. 2:4
Ps. 62:6–8

Eph. 4:14
Ps. 1
John 15:4–5

173 Stability lies even more in your *fidelity to your commitment* to the monastic ideal: in your obedience in everything that is asked of you. It also lies in your attachment to the monastic family to which you spiritually and canonically belong; and to this Rule that you read and follow. It lies in your basic attachment to Jerusalem as it is today and as it will become tomorrow; in fidelity to the community that accepts you, selects you and assigns you your mission; in the trust you place in your prior; in your word given once and for all.

By your perpetual vows you attach yourself to your Fraternity for ever, this in itself being an act of humility, for you are not setting out to conquer the world; an act of faith, for your true pilgrimage is inwards to the centre of your heart; an act of love, for now your life is bound up irrevocably with that of your brothers, and committed to the same ideal of sanctity. Once this commitment has been made, understand it binds you till death.[2] For it is a commit-

---

[2] St Basil, *Longer Rule* 7, 14, 36.

ment of love celebrated between the Fraternity and
yourself like the betrothal of those whose love is
stronger than death; a love no flood can quench, nor
torrents drown.

Bear fruit in perseverance,
Never tire of marvelling about God.
Witness to the power of fidelity.
And let it be your glory, Lord,
That my weakness in your service holds firm![3]

174   *Ecumenism* is another constituent part of Jerusalem. The name you bear will remind you that Christ
died near the Holy City for the salvation and unity of
all, and that your life too, like his, brother and sister
of Jerusalem, should harbour this same passion for
unity.   John 11:52
    The monk is a man looking first for his own unific-
ation. Live ecumenism at the centre of your own life:
a unified man brings unity. Live ecumenism within
your own community by joyful and constructive
acceptance of its variations. Live ecumenism in the
context of world Christianity, so that all the still separated disciples of Christ may become more and more
like brothers. The most effective form of ecumenism
is prayer.
    Be careful, too, to have a true heartfelt concern for
communion with all the sons of Abraham, Jews and
Moslems who, like you, are worshippers of the one
God and for whom Jerusalem is also a holy city. Do
not hesitate to pray throughout your life for the day
when there will be only one flock and one shepherd.
And let Christ's passionate desire be the passion of
your own monastic life! He consecrated himself for
you so that you too might be truly consecrated. Only
the unity of the sons of God can reveal the mystery   John 10:16;
of the true God to the world.   17:19, 23
    Jerusalem restored! The city, one united whole, to
which the tribes come up, the tribes of the Lord.   Ps. 122
    Believers are never so united as when they worship

[3] William of St Thierry.

at the heart of the same God; as when they acknowledge one another as brothers, since they see one
another as sons of the same Father. Let the words of
Jesus's last prayer to be offered inside the Holy City
be tirelessly repeated in your heart: May they all be
one!

175 The Fraternities of Jerusalem are made up of *monks
and nuns* bearing the same name, living in the same
spirit and following the same Book of Life. Thus God
allows a twofold witness of purity and friendship, and
each Fraternity finds itself enriched by grace of its
opposite number. They share a common vocation.

Remember, though, that in no sense and never is
a mixed monasticism envisaged. For that would be
completely unrealistic. Monks and nuns function
independently, each with their own government and
separate dwellings, and respecting each other's charisms they develop with no sort of interference as
regards discernment of vocations or the routine of
daily life. The nuns have their prioress. The monks
have their prior. Let the prioress keep her autonomy
and the prior his independence. The better their
specific prerogatives are defined and respected, the
better the understanding and the stronger the unity
between them.

The autonomy of cenobites and of hermits should
similarly be respected.

176 The daily celebration of the Eucharist and the
sharing of the same doctrinal instruction will create a
living bond of communion between the brothers and
sisters. And what could be more essential? Guided by
the same Word, nourished by the same Body, bearing
the same name and living the same spiritual ideal, the
brothers and sisters will become serene and joyful
Matt. 19:12 witnesses to the kingdom that is to come.

You will need to be open-minded and understanding to accept this close, yet independent, parallel
road. Harmony never comes at the outset. Nor readiness to have one's methods questioned. But if you

learn how to acquiesce, to live and love what God has given you in this, you will find this complementary arrangement a cause for rejoicing, conversion, external evangelization and inward sanctification. By it, humbly and gladly, you will bring the world a twofold witness of purity and friendship.

Thank the Lord every day for the grace that he has given Jerusalem in this. Indeed this is a great mystery. I mean, it applies to Christ and the Church.[4]

177   Our Fraternities are specially consecrated to the *Blessed Virgin Mary.*

You should be able to turn to her each day.

Virgin, wife and mother, she will teach you the secret of the wedded state, the meaning of virginity, the nature of fatherhood and the mystery of motherly love.

Because she is the mother of fair love, she will help you to love.

Because she is the light of prayer, she will help you to pray.

Because she loves the mystery of silence, she will introduce you to its secret.

Because she loves you, you too must learn to love her.

With Mary, do all that Christ bids you and, like her, be happy! Mary leads the way for the Jerusalem of today towards the new Jerusalem.   John 2:5

Jerusalem, turn your eyes to the East and see the joy that is coming to you from God.   Baruch 4:36

So I shall get up and go through the city; have you seen him whom my heart loves?   S. of S. 3:12

I saw the holy city, the new Jerusalem, coming down from heaven as beautiful as a bride adorned for her husband.   Rev. 21:2

Pray much to the holy, merciful and immaculate Mother of God.

At Bethlehem Mary gave you the eternal God

[4] Biblical references for this paragraph in sequence: Isa. 60:4; Joel 3; Ps. 45; Zeph. 3:14–18; Zech. 9:9, 16–17; Eph. 5:32; Acts 1:13–14; Luke 8:1–3.

become a little Child. At the foot of the cross she stood near her Son while he died for you. In Jerusalem she will reveal the true face of Emmanuel to you.

15 Joy

178   Joy has been given us to live by and bear witness to the same. So we should strive to open our hearts to receive it and let it radiate from us.

God is Joy: in your presence, unbounded joy, and at your right hand, everlasting pleasures. Being sons of God we are consequently sons of joy. Our hearts rejoice in him, we trust in his holy name. Thus each one of us is begotten by his joy and promised to his gladness.

Ps. 16:11; 33:21
Isa. 35:1–10

The basis of our joy is, first of all, the *Father's mercy*, that does not will the death of a sinner but that he be converted and live; the Father who invites the whole world to feast and rejoice at the first sign of our returning to him. So be happy at the thought of this loving and forgiving presence, making you sing to him, You have always helped me: I sing for joy in the shadow of your wings!

Ezek. 18:32
Luke 15:23–4
Ps. 63:8

179   Besides this, our joy comes from knowing that *Christ's presence* will be with us to the end of time. We have not seen him, yet we love him; we do not see him, yet we exult in indescribably glorious joy, sure of obtaining salvation of our souls through him. He who came to bring us the Good News has revealed his love to us, so that his joy may be in us and that our joy may be complete, and that hence we ourselves may have this fulness of his joy. Abide in Christ's joyfulness as he travels beside you, bearer of a gladness that no one can take from you. You have good reason to love him!

John 16:33
1 Pet. 1:8–9
Mark 1:15
John 15:11;
17:13, 16:22
S. of S. 1:4

Finally, our joy is confirmed by the *grace of the Holy Spirit* who is himself jubilant joy in the heart of the

Trinity. He is the bearer of joy, radiating joy. He *is* joy. *True* joy.

For there is such a thing as the joy of the Holy Spirit, able to make us drunk with joy. Now this Spirit has been given to us, filling us with his riches, of which the first, after love, is joy. So do not grieve the Holy Spirit within you by letting the world's miseries depress you. Child of God, friend of Christ, bearer of the Spirit, live by the joy of your God.

Rom. 14:17
Acts 2:15
Isa. 29:9
Gal. 5:22
2 Cor. 7:10

180   The brotherly life that makes a community gathered in his name a living sign of his presence, becomes in turn a source radiating joy. See how good, how pleasant it is to live like brothers all together. Love expands, mutual trust brings peace, the common life gives joy. That we should radiate the trinitarian presence is what God and men expect of us, as it is written: Rejoice without end in the Lord, yes, rejoice! The serenity of your life should impress everyone. The Lord is near. Put all care aside.

Ps. 133:1
Phil. 4:4–6

By living in love bring about a blossoming of joy in each of your brothers and in yourself. Together with your brothers, let the expansion of your communal joy become the sign of God's presence, God who wants to renew you by his love and dance for you with shouts of joy as on a feast day. Nothing is more saddening than quarrels, distrust, murmuring, jealousy. Conversely, forgiveness, helpfulness, compassion and humility are sources of gladness. To live in joy means living at unity, filling up our own cup of happiness by thinking and feeling alike. Ask daily for each brother in the community the grace of joy. Ask and you will receive and your joy will be perfect.

Zeph. 3:17
Phil. 2:2
John 16–24

181   Never forget though that *joy is the daughter of sacrifice*.

True joy springs from effort, trial and suffering, just as Easter joy came from the cross. Take it as a supreme joy, brothers, to have to face every kind of trial. In difficulties, insults, vexations, persecutions, rejoice, for your reward is great in heaven. There is no deep joy without self-sacrifice and without an active sharing in the cross of Jesus. Jas. 1:2
Matt. 5:12
1 Cor. 2:2
Gal. 6:14

In so far as you share in Christ's sufferings, be glad, so that, when his glory is revealed, you also may be full of joy and gladness. Fasting, chastity, vigils, forgiveness of offences, are attitudes of heart, mind and body that gladden the soul. And joy for the man of upright heart. 1 Pet. 4:13
Ps. 97:11

Even if God's punishments are not at first always a subject for rejoicing, serenity invariably follows on self-denial. There may be tears in the evening, but joy comes in the morning. You have turned my sorrow into dancing, you have stripped off my sackcloth and wrapped me in gladness. Give yourself to ascesis and you will know perfect joy. Heb. 12:11
Ps. 30:6, 12

Bare your shoulder to the burden of discipline and do not let its bonds make you impatient, for in the end you will find rest in it and it will change into joy. If you, too, can say one day that you no longer seek yourself, you will lead the happiest of lives. For then your whole life will be lived in expectation of true happiness. As it is said: the hope of righteous men is all joy. Ecclus. 6:25–8
Prov. 10:28

182   Our daily life should be illuminated and sustained in its struggles by the *ultimate perspective of bliss*. It is good to be able to repeat with St Paul that the sufferings we now endure bear no comparison to the glory as yet unrevealed which is in store for us; and that our troubles, which are slight and short-lived, are preparing us for an eternal glory outweighing them by far. Our whole life is a journey towards eternal happiness! One day we shall all reach Zion, shouting for joy, eternal bliss transfiguring our faces, with joy and gladness as our companions. How can we as monks, looking forward to the certainty of this meeting with God and trying to anticipate that Day, do otherwise than sing as we journey day by day, like the psalmist going up to Jerusalem, How glad I was Rom. 8:18
2 Cor. 4:17

Isa. 35:10
Ps. 122:1 when they said to me: Let us go to the house of the
Lord!

Live then according to God's promise: Be glad and
rejoice for ever and ever because I am going to create
Jerusalem which is Joy and her people who are Gladness. I shall rejoice over Jerusalem and exult in my
Isa. 65:18–19 People.

Take courage, Jerusalem, he who gave you that
name will console you.

Jerusalem, turn your eyes to the East and see the
Baruch 4:30–6 joy that is coming to you from God.

*Fraternités de Jérusalem
13 rue des Barres
75004 Paris*